THE
Glamorous
GIRLS' BOOK

Written by
Sally Jeffrie and Veena Bhairo-Smith

Illustrated by Nellie Ryan

Cover illustrated by Jo Goodberry

Edited by Liz Scoggins, Sally Pilkington and Lauren Taylor

THE Glamorous GIRLS' BOOK

Buster Books

For the lovely Kate Jeffrie

This paperback edition first published 2013.
First published in Great Britain in 2012 in a hardback edition titled
The Glamorous Girls' Book by Buster Books, an imprint of Michael O'Mara
Books Limited, 9 Lion Yard, Tremadoc Road, London SW4 7NQ.

The material in this book was taken from two titles previously published
by Buster Books: *The Girls' Book of Glamour* and *The Fabulous Girls' Book*.

www.busterbooks.co.uk

A CIP catalogue record for this book is available from the British Library.

ISBN: 978-1-78055-197-5

2 4 6 8 10 9 7 5 3 1

Printed and bound in December 2012 by
CPI Group (UK) Ltd, 108 Beddington Lane, Croydon, CR0 4YY, United Kingdom.

Papers used by Michael O'Mara Books are natural, recyclable products made
from wood grown in sustainable forests. The manufacturing processes conform to
the environmental regulations of the country of origin.

CONTENTS

NOTE TO READERS

This book is brimming with glamorous ideas for you to explore. From fabulous fashion tips and cool crafts to confidence boosters and simple cookery, you'll be feeling ready to take on the world.

Being glamourous is not about how many clothes or how much money you have. It's about being happy with yourself inside and outside.

The most glamorous girls use their best common sense at all times. Don't do anything that makes you feel uncomfortable. Be careful with sharp objects, kitchen utensils and hot liquids, and get permission from the appropriate adult. Stay within the law and local rules, and be considerate of other people.

The most important thing you should do with this book is ...
... HAVE FUN!

How To Make A Good First Impression

First impressions usually last so follow these pointers to make everyone's first thoughts of you the best they can be.

- ❤ Remember to introduce yourself and ask the other person's name.

- ❤ Look them in the eye, smile and remember to speak clearly.

- ❤ Pay attention to what the other person is saying.

- ❤ Ask questions about their interests and hobbies.

- ❤ Just be yourself.

How To Take A Compliment

There's nothing like receiving dozens of compliments to build up your confidence, even if you flush with embarrassment at first. It's a good idea to use these top tips for the next time a friend says something lovely about you.

- ❤ DO smile and say 'thank you'.

- ❤ DO be modest.

- ❤ DO compliment them in return.

- ❤ DON'T frown, mumble or look at the floor.

- ❤ DON'T just say 'I know'.

- ❤ DON'T disagree.

HOW TO DESCEND A STAIRCASE

A vital part of glamour is impressing people and there's no better way than with a grand entrance. Whether you're arriving at a ball or just trying to wow your friends at school, descending a staircase with style and grace can make a great impression. Here are some pointers for making the best entrance ever - and avoiding any embarrassing slips, trips or falls.

❤ Pause at the top of the stairs and gaze confidently around the room for a few seconds until everyone turns to look at you. This way you are sure to make maximum impact.

❤ Discreetly check the staircase ahead for any obvious hazards or obstacles before you take a step.

- If you are in a long ballgown, make sure you lift up the bottom of your dress so you don't tumble.

- Lift up your chin, smile and then lightly grip the handrail to help you keep your balance.

- Step gracefully out on to the first stair, keep smiling and remember not to look at your feet.

- Walk carefully and steadily down the stairs until you reach the bottom. Voilà.

How To Air Kiss

Make sure you make a cool impression when you bump into friends. It's time to perfect the celebrity-style 'air kiss'.

Start by making sure that you look delighted to see your friend. Smile and widen your eyes and exclaim at how lovely she looks, saying 'Darling', 'Honey' and 'Sweetheart' at the same time. Finally swoop towards her and almost touch her left cheek with yours and then her right cheek while saying 'Mwah' loudly each time.

How To Flatter A Friend

An essential part of glamour is making other people feel great about themselves, too. So don't just focus on yourself - add an aura of niceness to your personality. Remember to compliment your friends and classmates on their best qualities and you'll soon see how good it makes them feel about themselves.

Things You Should Say:

- ❤ 'Your hair looks lovely.'

- ❤ 'I love your drawings.'

- ❤ 'You're really talented.'

- ❤ 'That really complements your eyes.'

- ❤ 'You've got really nice handwriting.'

- ❤ 'You're so well co-ordinated.'

- ❤ 'You're so good at sport.'

Things You Shouldn't Say:

- 💜 'That's so last season.'

- 💜 'Get with the programme!'

- 💜 'You shouldn't wear that colour again.'

- 💜 'What on Earth are you wearing?'

- 💜 'Hahahahahaha.'

How To Make Your Own Lip Gloss

To give your lips a delicious glow you need a great lip gloss. Don't spend a fortune - make your own.

What you need:
- 30ml (2 tablespoons) of petroleum jelly
- 5ml (about 1 teaspoon) of runny honey
- 2 drops of food flavouring - peppermint, strawberry or vanilla are particularly good
- Ultra-fine glitter from an art and craft shop (optional).

Mix all the ingredients together until thoroughly blended. Transfer the mixture to a small, clean pot or jar and apply regularly to your lips for a stunning shine.

How To Customize Your School Uniform

I t is possible to express your own style even if you have to wear a school uniform. Here's how to do it without risking a detention.

💜 Find out about your school's uniform policy and check it thoroughly for any loopholes. How much you'll be able to customize your uniform depends on how strict your school is. Don't go too far and risk detention!

💜 Most schools don't insist you wear a particular size or length - within reason. For instance, if you like loose clothes then opt for a blazer in a slightly larger size so it hangs in a baggy style.

💜 If you have to wear a tie, think about how you'll wear it - perhaps you'd like it very short with a fat knot, or maybe you'd prefer it long with a thin knot. Experiment.

💜 Check out sales of second-hand school uniforms - most schools have them yearly. Designs of school uniforms subtly change over the years and you might prefer the vintage style of a second-hand item to the new ones currently in the shops.

❤ Investigate which items you're allowed to choose for yourself and then really express your taste with them. For instance, backpacks can be transformed with a clutch of decorative key rings, shoes can be updated by adding coloured laces and a new hairstyle can be created with different clips and grips.

❤ If your school only insists that you wear certain colours rather than specific items of clothing, you're really in luck. You'll be able to experiment with a wide variety of great styles while sticking to the colour rule.

❤ Get to know when your teachers are most likely to enforce uniform rules. For instance, it may be fine to look a bit more casual at break time so long as you smarten up for assembly.

Remember - it's definitely your personality, not what you wear, that really matters.

How To Eat Your Way To Beautiful Skin

L otions and potions are great and smell lovely, but the very best way to get beautiful skin is from the inside out, which means eating a skin-friendly, healthy diet.

Water Works
You should drink plenty of water throughout the day to keep your skin clear and bright. Aim for about six glasses a day to keep your levels topped up and avoid any fizzy drinks, which are full of sugar.

Fresh And Fruity
You should try to eat at least five portions of fresh fruit and vegetables every day. Skin-friendly superfoods include carrots, broccoli, apricots, strawberries, watercress and oranges. They're great for the rest of your body, too.

Great News!
Experts can't find any evidence to link eating chocolate with having problem skin, so you can still indulge in the occasional choc-attack.

PERFECT DAILY MEAL PLAN

It's important not to skip meals
- a regular, healthy diet can work
wonders on your skin and give
you lots of energy.

BREAKFAST: Start with a glass
of fresh juice, wholegrain cereal
with chopped banana and milk,
followed by toast and honey.

LUNCH: Make a cheese or ham
sandwich on wholemeal bread
with salad followed by yogurt
and fruit.

DINNER: Go for grilled chicken
and a baked potato with fresh
vegetables, followed by fresh fruit
salad with yogurt and nuts.

SNACKS: Don't go hungry between
meals. If you feel peckish try
a healthy snack to keep you
going. Fruit, nuts, vegetable sticks,
crackers, yogurt or a slice of
wholemeal toast are far better for
you than sweets or crisps.

How To Get The Shiniest Hair Ever

If your hair's looking dull and dirty, it's time to take some action. A few extra treats will soon have it back to its shiny, healthy best.

Be A Water Baby
Just as drinking lots of water can help brighten your skin, a good dose of H_2O can keep your hair shiny, too.

Little And Often
If your hair is looking less than glamorous, lather up regularly with a mild shampoo to keep the dirt at bay.

Shampoo Dry Hair
If your hair is ultra-dirty try applying the shampoo straight on to dry hair – leave for a couple of minutes before you get to work with water.

GET CONDITIONING

Condition your hair regularly to guarantee silky, shiny tresses.
This easy recipe works really well and saves you cash.

What you need:
- 5ml (1 teaspoon) of runny honey
- A dash of vinegar
- 50ml (3 tablespoons) of evaporated milk.

Mix the ingredients together in a bowl and cover your hair.
Wind a warm towel around your head and wait for 20
minutes before rinsing thoroughly. The milk will cleanse your
hair, while the honey nourishes and the vinegar adds a gloss.

RINSE, RINSE, RINSE

Rinse your hair under the shower until the water runs
completely clear to be sure no shampoo or conditioner is left
behind - it will just make your hair look dull and drab again.

GET BRUSHING

Groom your hair once or twice a day to remove built-up dirt
and dead skin cells. Brush thoroughly before you wash your
hair to allow the shampoo to move easily through it.

There's no point brushing your shiny hair with
a dirty brush. Wash your brushes and combs
regularly in a bowl of warm water with a dollop of
shampoo and leave them to dry on a towel.

How To Turn Bathtime Into A Relaxing Treat

This bubble-icious bath is best taken just before bed. Get all your chores and homework done first so you can R-E-L-A-X.

Set the Scene

💜 Make sure the bathroom is warm with clean towels ready.

💜 Have a cup of juice or water nearby, ready to sip as you soak.

💜 Put on some music and light a scented candle - a lavender one smells especially delicious and is very relaxing.

💜 Add a little scented bubble bath or oil to the running water - but take care not to leave the bath slippery for the next person.

The heads of flowers floating on the surface of the water add a serious touch of glamour.

R-E-L-A-X

Sink into the water and lie there for 20 minutes. Rest your head on a bath cushion or a rolled-up towel and breathe slowly and deeply. Lie there and imagine all the worries of your day dissolving into the water.

Afterwards

Pat your skin dry with a warm, soft towel. Smooth your skin with a little scented body lotion, taking special care of really dry areas like knees and elbows. Pull on your PJs and head straight for bed. Sprinkle a couple of drops of lavender oil on to your pillow to help you drop off.

How To Make Your Own Bubble Bath

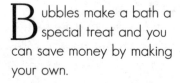

Bubbles make a bath a special treat and you can save money by making your own.

Mix together 120ml (½ cup) of baby shampoo, 180ml (¾ cup) of water and a few pinches of salt. Finally, stir in a few drops of essential oil (lavender, lemon or peppermint are especially nice).

Pour the mixture into a pretty bottle. Try to find a plastic one, which won't break if you drop it. Decorate the bottle with stickers and a cute ribbon and enjoy your bath!

How To Quickly Smooth Away Dry Hands

K eep a tube of hand lotion by your bedside at all times and remember to apply a drop every morning and evening to keep your skin soft and smooth. But, if your skin is still very dry, try this mini treat:

1. Run yourself a warm bath.

2. Cover your hands in oil – olive oil from the kitchen is fine, although manicurists prefer almond oil. Take the time to rub the oil into your nails, too, as it will help them to grow stronger.

3. Smooth on lots of rich hand lotion – it'll create a barrier around the oil and encourage it to sink into your skin.

4. Now soak in the bath for 10 minutes, allowing your hands to rest in the water.

5. When you get out of the bath, gently rub your hands dry, then apply a few more drops of hand lotion. Now your hands should be beatifully soft.

How To Convince People You're A Hand Model

Just having beautiful hands isn't enough – you have to act the part properly as well. Following these tips will help convince your friends that your hands are your fortune and provide you with a ready-made excuse for avoiding all sorts of boring tasks.

- ❤ Refuse to do anything that might damage your hands. This can include doing the washing-up (dries out the skin), writing essays (you could get ink on your fingers) and taking the dog for a walk (the dog's lead could cause calluses to form on your hands).

- ❤ Gather together a handful of props like a lipstick, a cup of coffee and a box of washing powder. Get your best friend to take close-up pictures of your hands holding the props – just like in the adverts. Mount the results in a photograph album and voilà: your very own portfolio to show people.

Practise hand-modelling poses whenever anyone's around. Don't just pass your mum a magazine she wants to read - strike a 'hand pose' as you do it.

♥ Wear white cotton manicure gloves to protect your hands at all times.

♥ Take up music lessons. Playing a musical instrument helps to encourage steady hands - vital for photographic shoots, which can go on for hours.

♥ Insist that you have jelly for pudding after every meal. Hand models say the gelatine in it is good for strengthening nails.

♥ Change the colour of your nail polish each night - after all, you need a new look for every single photoshoot.

♥ Get your parents to insure your hands for a million pounds.

How To Persuade Your Best Friend To Lend You Her Clothes

A clever way to DOUBLE the size of your wardrobe is to share clothes with a friend. However, if your most stylish friend doesn't seem keen on letting you borrow her clothes, you'll need to learn how to use the art of persuasion ...

- ♥ Compliment her on her brilliant taste in clothes and stress how much you'd love to be as well-dressed as her.

- ♥ Explain that you'd like to experiment with clothes more but you don't have enough money to buy lots of new things.

- ♥ Offer to let her take her pick of your wardrobe if she'll lend you something in return. (If you haven't got many clothes wait until your friend has agreed to swap before you let her see the contents of your wardrobe.)

Be very careful with your friend's clothes – if you ruin them she'll never let you borrow anything again.

❤ Promise to wash and iron her clothes before you give them back to her. You will even dry-clean them, if necessary.

❤ Promise to give her clothes back on an agreed date – and stick to that date to ensure she's happy to swap with you again.

How To Apply Eyeshadow

When you're ready to start experimenting with make-up it's a good idea to practise your technique at home before you unleash your new look on the world. Look for flattering, natural shades in a powder finish to highlight the colour of your eyes:

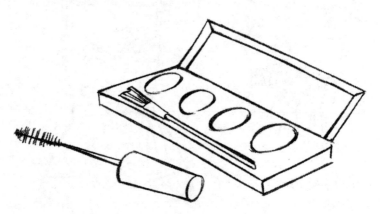

BLUE EYES ... pastel pinks or peach shades

BROWN EYES ... olive green or golden brown

GREEN EYES ... lilac or gold

HAZEL EYES ... greys or mauve.

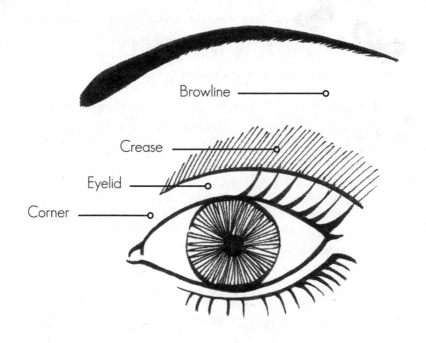

Browline ———————o

Crease ———————o

Eyelid ———————o

Corner ———————o

Make sure your parents are happy for you to try make-up and then start saving your pocket money for your favourite colours. Most make-up ranges offer eyeshadows in sets of three shades, which makes it even easier to find great colours to suit you.

Start with a little of the palest shade to highlight your brow line. Next brush the medium shade across your eyelid, avoiding the inner corner. Then use the darkest colour around the crease of your eye socket to define the shape of your eye. Blend the colours where they meet. Easy peasy.

How To Deal With Zits

Even supermodels sometimes get spots. However, with a little know-how you can help a spot to heal quickly and make it almost invisible to the naked eye. Here's the low-down ...

How To Cure A Spot

Firstly, NEVER squeeze a spot - it'll just look even more red and inflamed. What's more, you'll risk pushing the infection deeper into your skin and it may leave a permanent scar.

1. Wash your skin thoroughly and pat dry with a clean towel.

2. Wrap an ice cube in a clean hanky and hold it over the spot for a minute or two - it'll help bring down the swelling.

3. Dip the end of a cotton bud into some diluted tea tree oil (available from your chemist) and dot a tiny amount directly on to the spot.

4. Leave it alone to get better.

> If you keep getting spots in the same area, check they are not being triggered by contact with a telephone, cycle helmet or sunglasses, which aren't spotlessly clean. Check they are not caused by leaning on your hands.

How To Use Concealer

Concealers are a great way to cover spots and blemishes so your skin looks perfect. You can buy them from the make-up counter at most chemists and department stores. Don't choose one that's darker or lighter than your natural skin-tone - you'll draw more attention to the problem.

1. If the spot's dry and crusty, apply a little petroleum jelly first to soften it.

2. Apply the concealer to the spot using a clean cotton bud. (Don't apply concealer on areas around the spot that don't need it or you'll just create a 'halo effect'.)

3. Pat some face powder over the concealer to set it and help it stay put all day long.

Don't apply concealer with your fingers or you'll risk spreading infection.

Important Information

If you feel you might be suffering from acne rather than just the occasional spot, make an appointment with your family doctor to ask for advice.

HOW TO MAKE YOUR OWN BODY GLITTER

This fabulous gel can be smoothed on to your body to make your skin shimmer. You can even smooth it through your hair for a gorgeous night-time glow.

What you need:
- 5ml (1 teaspoon) of petroleum jelly
- 20ml (4 teaspoons) of aloe vera gel. Aloe vera gel is used to soothe sunburnt or sore skin – it's easy to find in chemists and healthfood stores
- Ultra-fine glitter (try art and craft stores)
- A small jar. Baby food jars or spice pots are ideal. Make sure they are thoroughly washed out in soapy water
- A small bowl
- A spoon.

How To Make It:

1. Spoon the aloe vera gel into the bowl. Add the petroleum jelly to make it a little thicker. Stir well.

2. Sprinkle a few pinches of glitter into your mixture. Stir well.

3. Smooth a little on to the back of your hand to see if you like the effect.

4. If it's too glittery, add a little more aloe vera gel. If it's not glittery enough, add an extra pinch of glitter.

5. Keep going until you like the results.

6. Spoon the mixture into your jar.

7. Smooth on the glitter whenever you like and glow, glow, glow!

HOW TO MAKE YOUR CLOTHES SMELL NICE

N ever, ever mix up clean clothes and dirty ones. Put dirty clothes straight into a laundry bag or basket, ready for washing.

- ❤ Air your clothes at the end of each day by putting them on a clothes hanger or the back of a chair near an open window.

- ❤ Pop your shoes on the windowsill at the same time - it will help to prevent any unpleasant smells developing.

- Put scented tumble-dryer sheets into your shoes when you're not wearing them to keep them smelling fresh.

- Unwrap a bar of scented soap and place it in the bottom of your wardrobe as an instant clothes freshener.

- Add a few drops of perfume to the final rinse when washing your favourite woollies. They'll smell gorgeous when you snuggle into them.

HOW TO BATHE LIKE CLEOPATRA

Cleopatra, the queen of ancient Egypt, was said to bathe in milk. You too can take a milk bath to soothe and soften your skin.

Just add two pints of whole milk to a tub of warm water. Swirl it around thoroughly, so that the water goes white. Hop in and have a good soak for at least 20 minutes. Rinse in clear cool water.

How To Jazz Up
A Boring Ponytail

A simple ponytail can be morphed into lots of new styles. With a little know-how and some practice you'll soon have the best ponytail around.

WRAP IT
Pull a strand of hair out of the ponytail. Wrap it around the top of your ponytail until the hair elastic is hidden. Secure in place with a hair clip.

KNOT IT
Separate your ponytail into six to eight strands. Twist each strand around and around until it forms a loose knot. Pin each knot randomly on to the back of your head.

CURL IT
Curl the ends of your ponytail with self-sticking rollers. Simply twist the rollers into slightly damp hair and leave them in until it's dry. When you remove the rollers, spritz the curls with hairspray to help them last for ages.

CRIMP IT

Pull a few random strands of hair loose from the ponytail. Crimp them with a heated crimping iron then let the tendrils fall around your face.

PLAIT IT

Simply plait a ponytail and secure the end with a hair elastic or pretty hair bobble.

ACCESSORIZE IT

Grab some pretty clips, hair snaps or other hair jewels and attach them all around the base of your ponytail. Alternatively, brush your hair into a low-slung ponytail at the nape of your neck. Tuck a few feathers – peacock feathers are fantastic – into the hair elastic.

DIP IT

Grab a sachet of temporary hair dye (the sort that washes out straight away – not permanent or semi-permanent). Follow the instructions on the packet carefully but only apply the dye to the ends of your hair. It should look as though your ponytail has been dipped in colour. Experiment with funky colours – black, red or orange are great for this look.

How To Do A Perfect Pirouette

Find a good place to practise your pirouette. Carpets are not good at all so try the tiles in your kitchen or bathroom. Make sure there's enough space that if you fall you won't crash into something and hurt yourself.

Start with your left foot turned out and the heel of your right foot against the toes. This is called 'fifth position'.

Lift your right arm as though you are hugging a beach ball to your chest and hold your left arm out to the side, slightly curved towards your body.

Now it's time for the difficult bit. Keep your back straight and in one graceful movement bend your knees outwards in a 'plié', push up on to the tiptoes of your left foot and bring your right foot up to your knee with your toes pointed.

At the same time use your momentum to spin clockwise.

When you have turned full circle, lower yourself off tiptoes on to your left foot and bring your right leg back into its original 'fifth position'. Always take the weight of your body on your supporting leg when you finish your pirouette.

GLAMOROUS TIP

It's a good idea to learn how to 'spot' so that you don't get dizzy spinning around. Practise slowly at first to get the technique just right. If you go too fast, you might hurt yourself.

Keep your eyes on one 'spot' on the wall. Slowly spin your body round, keeping your head in the same position until you can't turn any more. Then whip your head around at the last possible second to the same spot again while you continue to turn. Perfect.

How To Make
Soap-On-A-Rope

Hanging the soap up in the shower means it's always easy to find – it makes a great gift, too.

What you need:
- Three bars of white soap
- A cheese grater
- A bowl and jug
- Some rope or ribbon
- Waxed or greaseproof paper
- Rubber gloves
- Food colouring (optional).

How To Make It:

1. Grate the soap into a bowl.

2. Fill the jug with warm water. If you want to make coloured soap, add a few drops of your chosen

food colouring to the water - don't overdo it though, or you'll find your skin changing colour as you wash!

3. Add drops of the warm water slowly to the soap flakes until it's the consistency of thick porridge.

4. Pull on the rubber gloves and mix well with your hands.

5. Cut the rope or ribbon into your chosen length (30-40cm is ideal) and lay on to the waxed paper.

6. Pat the soap mixture around one end of the rope in a ball shape, making sure the rope is in the centre of the soap ball.

7. Once you're happy with the shape, leave the soap to dry for around 24 hours.

8. Tie a loop in the other end of the rope so that you can hang it up in the shower.

GLAMOROUS TIP

You can add a handful of other ingredients to the soap mixture to give it a touch of something special.

- ♥ Porridge oats turn a simple soap into an effective body scrub.

- ♥ Dried flowers look and smell very pretty.

- ♥ Grated lemon peel makes a refreshing soap that will really wake you up in the morning.

How To Get The Flutteriest Lashes

A slick of mascara is the best way to create a fluttering fringe to your eyes – especially if you have light-coloured hair and your lashes are harder to notice. Here's what you need to know:

Most mascaras are applied with a spiral brush at the end of a wand as this makes them quick and easy to use. Some contain fibres to add extra thickness and length to your lashes. For a girl on the go, waterproof mascara is the best choice. It will withstand tears, showers and swimming. However, remember you'll need a special make-up remover to take it off as it clings to your lashes more than ordinary mascara.

1. Start by applying mascara to your upper lashes first. Brush them downwards to begin with, then brush the lashes upwards from underneath. Use a tiny zigzag movement from side to side to prevent the mascara turning to lumps on your lashes.

2. With the tip of the mascara wand brush your lower lashes, using a gentle side-to-side technique. You can keep your hand steady by resting your elbow on a firm surface. If you've got a shaky hand, try holding the edge of a tissue under your eyelashes while applying mascara to prevent it smudging on to your skin.

3. Comb through your lashes with an eyelash comb to remove any small lumps of mascara. This will prevent your lashes from clumping together.

4. Take care not to blink while the mascara is still wet or your lashes will stick together.

5. Repeat the whole process once or twice more to create a really fluttery effect.

How To Work Out
Your Face Shape

D ifferent hairstyles suit different face shapes. The four main face shapes are oval, round, heart-shaped and square.

To work out what shape your face is, pull all your hair back from your face with a hairband. Look in a mirror and trace around the outline of your face with a lipstick (the sharp edge of a bar of soap will work well, too). Move away from the mirror and look carefully at the shape. Decide which shape your face is most similar to, then check out the description and choose from your ideal hairstyles. (Don't forget to clean the mirror afterwards!)

Oval
Any style suits an oval face so you can try really dramatic looks like ultra-short bobs and 'urchin' crops as well as long, straight hair.

Round

You would suit chin-length bobs. Soft layers or side partings will also look great on you.

Heart-Shaped

Try neat styles with flipped-up ends. Long wispy fringes, waves or short and spiky cuts would also work well for you.

Square

Go for soft layers, curls, side-swept partings or hair swept on to your face.

HOW TO MAKE YOUR
EYES LOOK BRIGHTER

If you're feeling tired and you've stared at a computer screen for too long or you're simply fighting off a cold, your eyes might start to look really red. Here's how to make them sparkle again with a simple three-step plan:

1. A lack of water can make your eyes look really tired so drink a litre and a half of water every day to banish redness.

2. Empty an ice cube tray into a sink of cold water and soak a flannel. Wring the cold flannel out, then lie down and place it over your eyes for five minutes. If the flannel gets too warm, soak it in the iced water again and repeat.

3. Apply a dot of pale, pearly eyeshadow on the skin at the inner corner of your eye and just above your pupil. This will make your eyes look wider and brighter even if you're still sleepy.

How To Make
A Bag Charm

G lam up a plain handbag or a boring old schoolbag with a safety pin bag charm. It couldn't be easier.

What you need:
- 30 safety pins, various sizes
- Beads of various sizes
- A piece of thin elastic - about 15cm.

Get Beading:

1. Open up a safety pin. Thread as many beads as you can on to the pin - don't forget to get creative with the pattern.

2. Close the pin carefully.

3. Repeat this process for as many safety pins as you have.

4. Knot a bead on one end of the piece of elastic.

5. Now start threading the beaded safety pins on to the elastic. Thread some through the top end of the pin, some through the bottom end and some through the middle.

6. Finish off with two beads, secured with a knot.

7. To secure the safety pin charm to your bag, tie the remaining end of the elastic thread around the base of your bag's handle.

HOW TO GIVE YOURSELF A MINI FACIAL

Every couple of weeks, set aside a bit of time to give yourself a relaxing salon-style facial at home. It'll help keep skin clean and super soft.

1. Smooth your skin with cleansing cream, gentle soap or facial wash. Leave on for one or two minutes to give it time to dissolve grime and make-up, then smooth away with a clean, damp flannel.

2. Massage a blob of facial scrub or some porridge oats over your skin to whisk away dead surface skin cells and clear blocked pores. Rinse away with warm water.

3. Fill a bowl with a kettleful of freshly boiled water (ask an adult to supervise this part). Then lean over the bowl, capturing the steam by placing a towel over your head. Stay there for five minutes to allow the steam to warm and soften your skin. Sensitive skins should skip this step.

4. Splash your face with warm water and pat dry.

5. Smooth on a home-made fruit face pack (see below).

6. Remove the mask with a clean tissue then rinse your face with warm water.

7. Finish with a splash of cool water to freshen your skin. Pat dry with a towel.

8. Dot your skin with moisturizer and massage it in to encourage a brighter complexion.

OILY SKINS: Crush six strawberries with a fork, smooth on to your face and leave for three minutes.

NORMAL/DRY SKINS: Crush a peeled banana with a fork, smooth on to your face and leave for five minutes.

How To Tell A Friend She's Made A Fashion Error

Too shy to tell a friend her top is on inside out or her shirt is buttoned up wrongly? Don't be – she'll be less embarrassed if a good friend tells her straight away rather than letting her walk around looking really silly all day long. And you never know when you might need her to do the same favour for you!

Don't actually point. This will only draw attention to the situation and embarrass her more.

Plan Ahead

Get together with your friends and make up some subtle hand signals to warn each other - you could tug on your earlobe or sing a snippet from your favourite song. That way you'll know that you have each other's backs just in case the worst happens.

If you haven't prepared in advance for a fatal fashion disaster then the best thing to do is to quickly grab your friend and tell her the error in your best quiet voice.

Handy Hints

- Compliment your friend on how well she handled the situation.

- Point out how great her taste in clothes is so who cares if anyone laughed?

- Change the subject as soon as you can.

Things To Avoid

- Any kind of laughter - this will only draw attention to the problem.

- Telling other people first - this is a quick way to end a friendship.

- Doing an impression of how embarrassed she was.

How To Customize A T-Shirt With Fabric Paints

Wear your art on your sleeve as well as on the rest of your T-shirt by getting nifty with some fabric paints. The easiest way to create your own T-shirt design is with fabric pens – they allow you to paint directly on to the fabric without any mixing or mess and you can get them from most art and craft shops.

1. You'll need a plain T-shirt. Choose a plain white or pastel-coloured one so that your design shows up really well.

2. Practise your design on a piece of paper first. You could try graffiti-style, designing your own logo or just drawing a simple, bold image like a face or a sun.

3. Now you're ready to paint your T-shirt. Put a piece of

thick paper or card inside the T-shirt so that the ink doesn't leak through from the front to the back.

4. Draw your image straight on to the T-shirt.

5. When you use fabric pens, you need to iron your finished design to help 'set' it. Check with an adult for advice or help before you do this.

> Once you've invested in a set of fabric pens, you can make use of them on lots of projects. Why not decorate bags or pillowcases?

How To Remove Ink Stains From Your Fingers

Oh no! You have an important birthday party to attend but your pen has leaked all over your hands. Inky fingers are okay for school but not so good for parties. Luckily it's easy to bleach away the stains with an ordinary lemon. Just cut the lemon in half and run the cut side over the ink stains. Wash your hands in gentle soap afterwards, then rub in some hand cream.

How To Stand Out From A Crowd

Everybody wants to feel like they fit in, but if you want to be truly fabulous, blending into the background simply isn't an option.

Look The Part

Dressing the same as your friends means you will always be grouped together and compared to one another. You will also always look the same, so no one will notice you. Make your look a little different by adding accessories, such as a ribbon belt threaded through the belt loops of your jeans (see page 76) or some funky jewellery.

You could even change the way you style your hair for a fresh new look. You don't have to be extreme and dye your hair green. Keep it simple. If your friends all wear their hair in high ponytails, wear yours in a low one arranged over one shoulder.

Take A Stand

Don't just agree with your friends for the sake of it. If you don't share the same views, don't be afraid to say so. Not having the same opinion doesn't mean you can't be friends. It's the differences between us that make life interesting.

A real friend will respect you for being different even when they don't agree with you – but make sure you respect their opinions, too.

Get A Hobby

Find a new and exciting hobby. Listening to a different type of music, reading books by different authors, or doing something you've never done before, such as joining a local drama group, can be great fun. It will give you something interesting to talk about, and you might even make some new friends along the way.

How To Convince People You're A Celebrity

❤ Wear huge sunglasses that practically cover your whole face even when you're inside the house eating your tea.

❤ Go to school with a film crew (your kid brother and his friends will do). Explain to your teacher that you're the subject of a brand new reality TV show.

❤ Carry a huge handbag with a dog the size of a hamster in it.

❤ Generously apply fake tan from top to toe until you are bright orange.

❤ Wear very silly shoes.

❤ Be unreasonable wherever you go. You could tell the dinner ladies you're on a special diet and can only eat blue food or tell your teacher you didn't finish your homework because you were practising your Oscar acceptance speech.

❤ Get your parents to tint the windows of the family car.

❤ Travel with an entourage (a group of friends) at all times to help you with any boring tasks.

❤ Persuade some friends to follow you around snapping photos of you constantly, and make sure you are overheard muttering "Pesky Paps!"

How To Persuade Your Parents To Let You Have Your Ears Pierced

If you really want to get your ears pierced you need to get permission first. It's worth planning how to get your parents on your side in advance.

- ❤ Before you start on your campaign to convince your parents, be sure you really do want your ears pierced – there are some great clip-on earrings available that look just as good.

- ❤ Do your research first. The more knowledge you have, the easier it'll be to persuade your parents.

Whatever you do, don't let a friend pierce your ears for you – it's unhygienic and you'll risk an infection.

❤ Offer to pay for it yourself or suggest it would be a great birthday present.

❤ Visit a couple of ear-piercing shops with your parents first. They will be able to check who would do the procedure and the equipment that's used. Let your parents choose which place they prefer.

❤ Don't burst into tears or throw a tantrum if they refuse.

❤ If they say no, leave it for a while and ask again. Perhaps you'll eventually be able to persuade them to set a date when they'll allow you to have your ears pierced.

How To Look After Newly Pierced Ears

Pierced ears might look good, but infected ears do not. Here's how to look after your newly pierced lobes properly:

- Make sure your first pair of earrings have gold posts (that's the part of the earring that goes through the hole). Gold posts are less likely to cause infection and swelling.

- When you first get your ears pierced, you should leave the earrings in for six weeks until your ears are completely healed. If you don't, your holes could close up and you'll have to go through everything all over again!

- Don't fiddle with your earrings during this healing process.

- Keep shampoo, soap and hairspray away from your ears.

- Apply antiseptic lotion to your ears morning and night - you should be given some by the person who pierced your ears.

- Wash your hands before applying the lotion to your ears with a clean cotton bud.

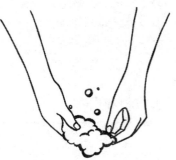

- Finally, rotate each earring once every morning and night.

WHAT IF YOUR EARS GET INFECTED?

An infected ear lobe may be swollen, red, warm and painful or oozing fluid. If you think one of your pierced ears may be infected, tell an adult. They can check with a doctor for advice on how to deal with it. You may be given special ointment to apply to your ears. Follow any advice carefully to ensure your pierced ears become healthy again.

How To Shampoo And Condition Your Hair Properly

*S*cientists have worked out exactly how you should wash and condition your hair. After experimenting on hundreds of people, they came up with the following instructions:

SHAMPOOING

- Dampen your hair with running water warmed to a temperature of precisely 36.7°C.

- Use exactly the right amount of shampoo - 6ml of shampoo for short hair, 8ml for medium length hair and 10ml for long hair.

- Lather hair for 28 seconds, rubbing it 20 times with your fingertips.

- Rinse your hair for 22 seconds in water that's 36.7°C.

- Repeat the whole process.

CONDITIONING

- 💜 Use 2ml conditioner for short hair, 4ml for medium hair and 6ml for long hair.

- 💜 Apply conditioner with a wide-toothed comb.

- 💜 Leave the conditioner to sink in for 57 seconds before rinsing with water at 36.7°C.

- 💜 Pat your hair dry with a towel to absorb excess water before leaving it to dry naturally.

You have been told!

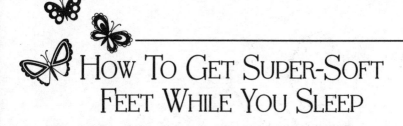

How To Get Super-Soft Feet While You Sleep

I ndulge your feet with the following treat once a week and they'll always be soft and smooth ...

1. Rub your feet with a layer of rich foot lotion. If you prefer, you can make your own by mixing 60ml (¼ cup) olive oil, 60ml (¼ cup) single cream and 20ml (1 tbsp) mayonnaise.

2. Pull on a pair of socks and head for bed.

3. Wash off the cream in the morning to reveal beautifully soft tootsies.

4. Don't forget to put the socks in the wash!

DID YOU KNOW?

❤ There are 26 bones in each of your feet.

❤ Each time your feet hit the floor, double the weight of your body impacts with the floor.

❤ Over 50% of people don't like their feet, often as a result of foot problems.

❤ Your feet contain around 250,000 sweat glands and they perspire more than any other part of your body. Each foot produces an egg-cup-full of sweat each day.

❤ In your lifetime, it's estimated that your feet will carry you 110,000km or almost three times around the world.

HOW TO GROW YOUR NAILS SUCCESSFULLY

If you regularly nibble your nails it's a hard habit to break, but well worth trying if you'd like to grow elegantly long and strong nails.

- ❤ Restrict yourself to biting the nails on just one hand and then on only one nail. You'll soon be inspired to grow out the bitten one.

- ❤ Regularly apply scented hand lotion or an anti-nail-biting cream. The unpleasant flavour will soon put you off gnawing your nails.

- ❤ If your parents and school allow it, try using stick-on nails for a few weeks so your nails have a chance to grow underneath.

Healthy Nails

Once you've broken a nail-biting habit follow these pointers to grow the perfect set of pinky tips. The secret to growing your nails is to make sure they are as strong as possible.

- ❤ Eat two portions of protein a day. Meat, fish, dairy, soya and lentils will all help your nails to grow strong and healthy.

- ❤ When you wash the dishes make sure you always wear washing-up gloves – soaking your hands in water weakens the nails.

- ❤ When your nails begin to grow keep them in shape with a nail file or an emery board to prevent them breaking.

- ❤ When filing, make sure your nails are dry, then gently smooth away any rough edges and file them into a nice, even shape.

- ❤ Never file down into the sides of your nails – it can lead to infection and seriously weakens them.

- ❤ Don't use your nails as a tool. Find the right tool for the job rather than risk having to grow your nail from scratch again.

- ❤ Once a week, soak your bare nails in a bowl of olive oil for 10 minutes. Then wipe away the excess oil with some cotton wool.

How To Shape Your Nails To Suit Your Hands

When you're filing your nails, make sure you bear in mind your overall hand-shape and pick a file-style that might suit you best.

- ❤ If you have small hands - go for almond-shaped nails.

- ❤ If you have quite short, wide fingers - aim for 'squoval'-shaped nails (which is just an oval with a squared-off tip).

- ❤ If you have large hands or wide nails try squared-off ends.

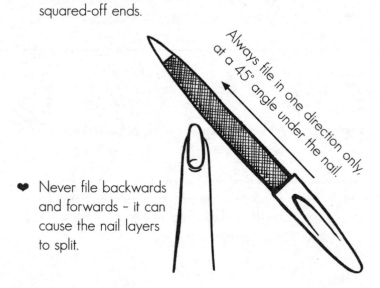

Always file in one direction only, at a 45° angle under the nail.

- ❤ Never file backwards and forwards - it can cause the nail layers to split.

How To Walk
With Confidence

The best way to make people think you're brimming with self-assurance and poise is to strut like a star. Follow these steps to get the best out of your stride.

1. Imagine that someone is pulling your head up with a long piece of string, push your shoulders back and smile.

2. Think of a fast-paced, lively song that you love and sing the tune in your head, or out loud if you prefer.

3. Gently start swinging your arms and walk along to the rhythm of your song, bouncing a little at the knees.

4. Heads will turn - just remember to smile and wave.

How To Pretend You've Got Freckles

If you have freckles, never try to hide them – they make you look naturally pretty and sun-kissed. If you're not lucky enough to have freckles, there's an easy way to fake them.

1. Start by making sure that your skin is really clean.

2. Choose a light brown eyebrow pencil if you have pale skin and a deeper shade if you have darker skin.

3. Sharpen the eyebrow pencil and dot a few freckles on to your face, concentrating them around your nose and cheeks.

4. To make your fake freckles look more realistic, apply different sized dots and soften the edges with a clean cotton bud.

5. Dust your skin with a little face powder to set them in place.

How To Get Rid Of Puffy Eyes

I f you've got a cold, hay fever or you're just really tired, try this de-puffing trick.

Stand a clean teaspoon in a glass of iced water. After a few minutes, remove it and hold the spoon against your closed eyes until they feel cooler and brighter.

How To Make Your Bedroom Skin-Friendly

C entral heating can draw the moisture out of your skin, leaving it dry and dull, but there's a simple way to prevent this happening.

Keep the air moist in your bedroom simply by placing a well-watered houseplant on your windowsill or by keeping a bowl of water near a radiator. The water will gradually evaporate and humidify the air, keeping your skin moist.

How To Exit
A Limo Gracefully

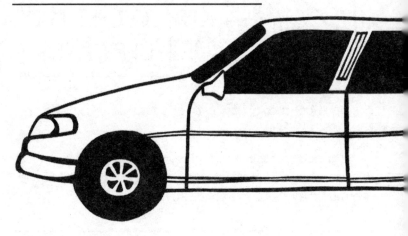

Once you're a celebrity you'll be invited everywhere - and a stretch limousine is definitely the best way to arrive. But when all your fans and photographers are waiting to see you it's important to learn how to get out of the car without falling over yourself.

1. Open the door on the pavement side and check there's room for you to get out easily. Don't let camera flashes distract you.

2. While staying seated swing both feet out on to the pavement. Use the door handle and the frame of the car to gently push yourself up in one smooth movement. Do not rush this stage.

3. Remember to tilt your head forward a little to avoid banging it on the door frame as you stand up straight.

4. Shake out your dress to make sure you haven't wrinkled it then turn towards your waiting fans to smile, wave and head for the red carpet zone.

5. Pause for a moment or two for the waiting photographers and film crews. Don't forget to strike a pose (see page 128).

6. Remember to stop and give a few quick autographs to some of your fans before heading in to your glamorous event.

HOW TO MAKE A RIBBON BELT

*J*azz up your tired old jeans with a pretty plaited belt made from lengths of colourful ribbon. Here's how to do it:

1. Look for ribbon that's about 2-3cm wide. You'll need enough to cut nine lengths, three times the circumference of your waist (this is the measurement around your waist).

2. Choose three different colours that all look good together.

3. Measure around your waist. Multiply this measurement by three - that's the length you should cut your ribbons to.

4. Take a strand of each colour. Tie them together in a knot at one end.

5. Lay the tied ribbons on a table and start plaiting. You can plait it loosely or tightly - it's up to you!

6. Tie a knot at the end of the plait.

7. Make two more plaits from the remaining ribbons. If you want to make a multicoloured belt you could even choose three new colours to plait.

8. Now plait the three plaits together to make a fat ribbon belt.

9. Secure the end of the fat ribbon plait with a knot.

10. Simply thread the belt through the loops of your jeans and tie the two ends together to secure. Time to show off your new style!

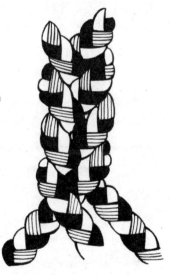

GLAMOROUS TIP

To create a more glamorous effect just cut the ribbon strands a little longer and leave the ends loose to flutter around. You could even add a selection of pretty, glittery beads for some extra sparkle.

HOW TO CREATE YOUR PERSONAL STYLE

F ollowing fashion slavishly can cost a small fortune. Be creative and come up with a brilliant style of your very own.

- ❤ Look for inspiration in magazines and on TV, then select the styles you like most.

- ❤ Pick and choose the things you like and imagine how you could combine them into a style of your own.

- ❤ Lay all your clothes out in your room and sort them into piles of things that suit you and things you'd like to adapt.

- ❤ Try changing the length or adding extra trimming to items that are old and dull.

- ❤ Experiment with unusual combinations and try layering or adding accessories.

- ❤ Scour second-hand shops for fabulous bargains that suit your style and pick them up cheaply. It's the greenest way to shop because you'll be recycling clothes.

How To Have The Prettiest Summer Feet

When summer comes around, it's time to get out the flip-flops and stop hiding your feet in trainers. Here's how to make sure your toenails are looking perfect to show off.

1. Get three pretty shades of polish that go well together (pastels work best).

2. Apply one coat of the first polish all over your toenails. Allow it to dry.

3. Grab the second shade and paint a dot of colour in the centre of each nail.

4. Take the last colour and place several dots around the centre, like the petals of a flower.

5. Allow the polish to dry.

6. Show off your new look by slipping on a pair of pretty flip-flops.

How To Host
A Spa-Style Party

Impress and pamper your friends by inviting them round for a relaxing and luxurious beauty evening at your place. Ask everyone to bring a dressing gown, flip-flops, hairbands, a mirror and a face cloth.

Get the mood right by covering seats and tables with white sheets. Use lamps or, better still, fairy lights to create a relaxing atmosphere and switch on some calming music.

Check out your local library for special CDs that are designed for relaxation (forest or ocean sounds are particularly mellow) for when you're having a foot massage – there are lots around.

Prepare some healthy spa-style snacks and drinks. Sparkling water or fruit juices look good in pretty glasses with colourful straws. Make special ice cubes to add to the drinks the day before. Pop slices of strawberry, lemon or lime into each section of an ice cube tray, then add water and freeze. A selection of fruit, popcorn and little sandwiches are good choices for mini-bites.

Snacks on cocktail sticks are a great idea – your guests will find them easier to pick up if they have wet nail polish.

Spa Treatments

Gather together a group of parents or friends to act as spa staff. Get them to set up separate 'beauty stations' offering different treatments. Create a poster board to outline which treatments are available, and let your guests pick the three they would like.

MAGICAL MASKS: For each mask, mix together a teaspoon of runny honey, three tablespoons of natural yoghurt and a few drops of lemon juice. Apply to clean skin and pop cucumber slices over the eyes. Relax for five minutes and rinse.

NIFTY NAILS: File away rough edges from nails with an emery board. Slick on clear nail polish, then sprinkle over some glitter while the polish is still wet. Seal in with a second coat of polish.

SENSATIONAL STRIPES: Get a tube of 'hair mascara' or some brightly coloured eyelash mascara. Comb it through dry hair for instant, wash-out highlights. This looks great if you concentrate the colour in the front sections of your guest's hair.

FRUITY FEET: Add a few drops of fruit-scented bubble bath to a large bowl of warm water. Get your guest to soak their feet for five minutes. Pat their feet dry then give them a foot massage using a few drops of olive oil or body lotion.

GLAMOROUS LASHES: Start by curling your friend's eyelashes with an eyelash curler. Gently does it – take care not to pinch her skin or pull on the lashes. Then slick on a coat of clear mascara to add extra definition.

And Finally ...

Before your guests leave take a photo of each of them to show the quality of your salon. Pour everyone a cup of bedtime herbal tea so they're sure to enjoy a good night's sleep when they get home.

How To Stop Chlorine In Swimming Pools Damaging Your Hair

Swimming is a fantastic way to get fit, but it can wreak havoc with your poor hair. That's because the water in most swimming pools contains a chemical called chlorine which kills germs in the water and makes it safe to swim in. But the trouble with chlorine is that it can make your hair dull, dry and unmanageable.

- ❤ Coat your hair with some conditioner, then pull on a swimming cap to protect it against the chlorine in the pool.

- ❤ If you're too vain to wear a swimming cap, make sure you wet your hair under the shower before you get into the water. That way your hair will already be soaked and as a result will absorb much less of the chlorinated water.

❤ Shampoo your hair as soon as you get out of the pool using a special swimmer's shampoo – this contains ingredients to remove the chlorine from your hair.

❤ Use loads of conditioner after swimming to guard against the drying effects of chlorine on your hair.

GLAMOROUS TIP

Chlorine can actually make blonde hair look a little green. If you have blonde hair and find this happens to you ask an adult to dissolve four soluble aspirin for you in a jug of water. Pour it over your hair and leave for five minutes, before rinsing. The juice of a lemon or a little vinegar in 500ml (2 cups) of water works pretty well, too.

HOW TO GROW OUT YOUR FRINGE

❤ Start wearing your fringe away from your face straightaway – use clips or a hairband to keep loose tendrils out of your eyes.

❤ Switch to a side parting so that your fringe still looks stylish as it grows out.

❤ Consider having some face-framing layers cut into the rest of your hair to help balance out your fringe as it's growing.

How To
Accessorize
Brilliantly

*Y*ou'll be surprised how many accessories you already have lying around at home. Anything from scarves and belts to brooches and bracelets can be used to add instant pizzazz to your wardrobe. Most of these ideas can be achieved with items you already own so you needn't spend any extra money.

❤ Tie the ends of a long scarf together and hook your left arm into the loop, then bring the scarf across your back and hook your right arm into the other end to make an instant shrug.

❤ If last year's coat is looking a bit bedraggled, jazz it up with a pretty brooch or a fabric flower. Pin it on to a lapel or somewhere just below your collar bone.

♥ If your hair is misbehaving why not just cover it up? Take a scarf or a pretty top and wrap it around your head like a turban or a bandana. For extra sparkle pin on a glamorous brooch just above your forehead.

♥ When a cold winter breeze is getting to you simply fold your scarf in half, loop it around your neck and slip the ends through the loop. This will cut out all the draughts and look super-stylish.

♥ Gather together all of the bangles and bracelets you own and put them all on at once - they'll be very eye-catching and make a great noise at the same time.

♥ A pretty silk or chiffon scarf can be used for lots of different things - knot it at the neck, tie it at the waist or loop it around your wrist and tie it in a stylish bow.

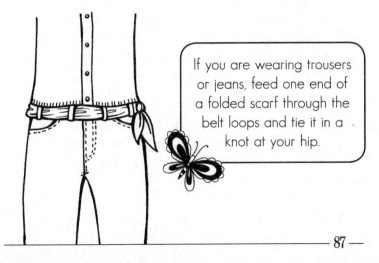

If you are wearing trousers or jeans, feed one end of a folded scarf through the belt loops and tie it in a knot at your hip.

How To Get Rid Of Tangles

If your hair's really tangled up you'll need to take special care when you try to untangle the knots or you'll risk badly damaging your crowning glory.

1. Start by smoothing lots of conditioner over your hair – use olive oil if you haven't got conditioner.

2. Try to separate the strands using your fingers. Start at the ends of the hair and work up towards the roots. Keep going until you get most of the large knots out. Hold the hair near the scalp with one hand and use the other to untangle. That way, when you brush, there will be less pulling (and less pain).

3. Take a wide-toothed comb and work it gently through your hair from the bottom upwards. Rub conditioner over the teeth of the comb to help it glide through the hair really easily.

4. Finally, comb through the hair with a fine-toothed comb until all the tangles are removed.

5. Rinse out the conditioner once your hair is knot-free. Then shampoo and condition again.

Try placing a rectangular silk scarf over your pillow while you sleep – it'll stop your hair fuzzing into knots.

How To Create Instant Glamour

For a speedy way to create an impression you can draw on a fake 'beauty spot'. Take a dark brown or black eyebrow pencil, depending on your skin tone, and apply a firm dot to your skin about 2cm from your top lip. Finally, pat on a little face powder to set it in place. Mesmerising glamour in moments!

How To French Plait Your Hair

This is a single braid that follows the curve of your head from the crown to the nape of your neck. A French plait is similar to a basic three-strand plait, except that you pick up extra strands of hair as you work your way down. As long as your hair is below chin-length you should be able to manage it. Get together with a friend and practise on each other.

HERE'S HOW TO DO IT:

1. Separate the hair from ear to ear, across the top of your friend's head. Gather the top section and divide it into three equal strands as though you're making an ordinary plait.

2. Start by crossing the right strand over the centre strand, then bring the left strand across, just as you would with a normal plait.

3. Before you plait the third strand scoop up an extra section of hair taken from the loose hair directly underneath.

4. Carry on plaiting, but from now on, add an extra section of hair to each strand as you go. Try to take a similar amount of hair each time to keep the plait even.

5. The plait will naturally follow the curve of her head as you pick up and include the new hair. Keep going until you reach the nape of the neck and all the hair from the sides of the head has been included. You should be left with a ponytail.

6. Finish by plaiting the rest of the hair to the ends and secure it with a pretty hair elastic or a ribbon.

How To Have
A Whiter Smile

Sparkling teeth and fresh breath are a real beauty boost. These tips will help give you a head-start.

❤ Brush your teeth twice a day to remove plaque. This is the sticky layer that builds up on teeth and it is the main cause of tooth decay.

❤ Brush for at least two minutes each time. Hum along to some music while you do it to help pass the time more quickly.

❤ Don't forget to brush your tongue as well as your teeth. This will clear the surface of old food and help prevent bad breath.

❤ An old toothbrush can't do its job properly, so change yours every three months, or sooner if the bristles are splayed.

❤ Use dental floss regularly to clean between your teeth where your toothbrush just can't reach.

❤ Visit your dentist twice a year to make sure your teeth are in perfect health.

❤ A natural remedy for sweet-smelling breath is to chew parsley leaves. They're rich in a chemical called 'chlorophyll' – Mother Nature's own deodorant.

❤ To help prevent tooth decay save sweets and sugary food and drink for an occasional treat.

❤ Keep your breath fresh by rinsing thoroughly with a mouthwash. Make your own using peppermint tea. Pour hot water over two tea bags and wait for it to cool before popping the cup in the fridge to chill.

Glamorous Tip

If you'd like really sparkling teeth you can even make your own whitening toothpaste. Baking soda has been used for years as a natural tooth whitener. It's really cheap and available in most supermarkets. Dip a dampened toothbrush into the soda, then gently brush your teeth to remove any stains and improve whiteness.

How To Order Food In A Restaurant

If your family is going out for a special meal remember these top tips and you'll be able to order your food with style and ease.

- ♥ Don't be afraid to ask what something is if you are unsure – it's much better than getting a nasty surprise on your plate.

- ♥ Some restaurants have loads of items on the menu. Don't bother to read the whole thing; pick a section you like the look of and choose from there.

Be prepared to try something new – you might enjoy it.

- ❤ It's perfectly alright to order a drink first if you need more time to decide. Don't be rushed into ordering too soon.

- ❤ Take a peek at what people are eating at other tables. If they look as though they're enjoying their meal choose the same dish.

- ❤ Try not to order too much. There's nothing worse than over-indulging and feeling terrible afterwards.

How To Get Rid Of Flaky Lips

Cold weather or nervous nibbling can lead to sore, dry lips. Here's a great way to make them better again.

- ❤ Slick your lips with petroleum jelly.

- ❤ Leave it on for ten minutes to soften any hard flakes of skin.

- ❤ Cover your index finger with a damp flannel and gently massage your lips. This will remove the petroleum jelly and the bits of dead skin at the same time.

- ❤ Rub a little petroleum jelly or lip salve into your lips frequently to prevent the problem happening again.

How To Make Your Own Jewellery Box

I f you have lots of pretty bracelets, beads and rings you need somewhere special to keep them. It's easy to turn an old carton or container into your own decorated jewellery box.

What you need:
- An empty cardboard box – an old chocolate box is ideal
- Various patterned papers to decorate with. Be as imaginative as you can. You could use pictures from old magazines and newspapers, old wrapping paper, used postage stamps, old musical scores or glittery stickers
- Liquid PVA craft glue – the sort that dries clear
- Fabric to line the box – anything from fun fur to velvet
- Scissors.

What To Do:

1. Cut up your pieces of paper.

2. Glue the pieces of paper to the outside of the box, making sure they overlap. Keep going until the whole box is covered. If you want your box to look old, now's the time to 'age' the paper. While the glue is drying simply leave a tea bag in water for a few minutes, then brush the tea over the surface of the box and leave it to dry.

3. Brush a layer of glue all over the surface of the box. This helps protect the box and makes it look shiny.

4. Once the glue's dry on the outside it's time to decorate the inside. Simply cut your chosen fabric to fit inside the base, sides and lid of your box and glue into place.

5. When it's dry, fill your new jewellery box with all your favourite trinkets.

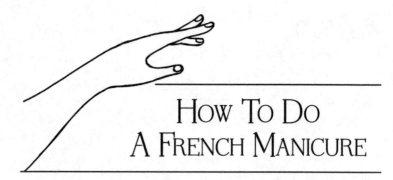

How To Do
A French Manicure

When it comes to nail trends, there's one look that never goes out of fashion and that's the French manicure. It leaves your nails looking clean, fresh and healthy, and it matches any outfit.

Here's How To Do It:

1. The classic French manicure uses two coats of pale pink polish. Look for a natural shade without any extra sparkly bits.

2. The best way to apply nail polish is in three strokes – one down the centre of the nail and one stroke either side. Apply two coats, giving each one plenty of time to dry.

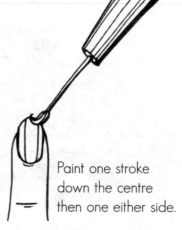

Paint one stroke down the centre then one either side.

To turn a French manicure into an
'American manicure', use a beige
polish instead of a pink one.

3. Now it's time to paint the tips
of your nails with a white polish.
Be careful not to overload the
brush or the varnish will flow down
the bristles too quickly for you to
control. Rest your hand on a firm
surface to keep your hands steady
and create a perfect finish.

Paint just the
tip white.

4. Once the white tips of your nails are dry, paint on a clear
topcoat of polish to seal in the colour and create a glossy
chip-free finish.

If you're feeling impatient you can
dry nail polish more quickly by
blasting your nails with a cold jet
of air from your hairdryer.

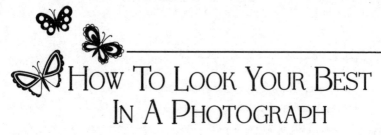

How To Look Your Best In A Photograph

M ake the most of any opportunity you get in front of a camera. Practise these useful pointers to make sure you always look your best.

- ❤ Brush your hair quickly in case it's sticking up and check that you don't have anything stuck between your teeth.

- ❤ Don't stand straight on to the camera. Turn your body slightly to one side, but keep your head facing forward for a more natural pose.

- ❤ Press your tongue to the roof of your mouth, lift your chin slightly as though you are stretching to look over a high garden fence and smile. This way you'll avoid any unflattering shadows under your chin.

♥ If your photographer is using a flash, widen your eyes a little just before the picture is taken so that you're not caught with your eyes closed.

♥ Try not to stand with your back to a light. You will only appear in silhouette, which will defeat the object!

♥ Don't look directly into the lens, look slightly to the side instead – this will help you to avoid 'red eye'.

♥ People always look good in a photograph when they are laughing – try to think of something funny just before the shot and you'll be caught at your best possible moment.

HOW TO MAKE
AN ACCEPTANCE SPEECH

*Y*ou've finally been nominated for an award and suddenly, out of all the nominees, the host announces that you're the winner! You have a limited time to make a dazzling acceptance speech so make sure yours is the one that people are talking about the next day. Follow these pointers to make the most of your moment at the mic.

- ❤ If possible choose a fun way to get on to the stage - run across the seats, cartwheel, crowd-surf or dance - anything, as long as you make a lasting impression.

- ❤ Remember to mention that it's an honour to be singled-out from such a wonderful group of nominees.

- ❤ Tears are fine, but make sure everyone can still hear you.

- ❤ Memorize a short list of the most important people to thank and then say 'Everyone else - you know who you are'.

- ❤ When the music starts playing, leave the stage immediately.

HOW TO SIGN AN AUTOGRAPH

B eing as fabulous as you are is sure to attract a few fans. These tips will make signing autographs a breeze.

YOUR SIGNATURE STYLE

Choose a writing style that suits your name. If you have a short name, make every letter count with bold swirls. If you have a long name, adding lots of swirls and detail will make it difficult to repeat every time, so concentrate on the first letters of your first and second name and trail off from there in a mysterious squiggle.

PRACTICE MAKES PERFECT

Practise your signature over and over again on a sheet of blank paper. It should flow naturally so that you don't need to think about it.

> To speed things up a bit, shorten your name like 'RPatz' and 'JLo'. This will stop your wrist getting sore.

How To Make Wellington Boots Work For You

Wellington boots might seem like a fashion no-no but with a little creativity and panache you'll be able to carry off a long walk through muddy fields easily. These tips are guaranteed to help you stay stylish.

- ❤ Look out for all the trendy wellie designs, from funky flowers to colourful rainbows – even celebrities are wearing them to brighten up their winter outfits.

- ❤ Alternatively you could funk up your old wellies by using water-proof pens or acrylic paints (see page 162).

- ❤ Always try to match your outfit to your boots. If you can co-ordinate with extra accessories, even better.

- ❤ Now even on the dullest day you'll be able to stay stylish and make the most boring wellies a fashion must-have.

How To Give Yourself A Face Massage

Just like every part of your body, your face will look better after a mini massage.

❤ Pour a few drops of olive oil into your hands and smooth it on to your face and neck.

❤ Use your fingers to stroke upwards from the base of your neck to your chin.

❤ Now stroke up one side of your face, then the other.

❤ Go around your nose and up towards your forehead.

❤ Stroke across your forehead from left to right, using one hand.

❤ Finish off by gently 'drawing' a circle around each eye using one finger.

How To Give A Great Interview

If you're about to give an interview to a magazine or TV journalist, it's important to prepare in advance. Good tactics can make a big difference and help you to leave a great lasting impression.

- ❤ When you meet the interviewer order a long, cool drink, such as a smoothie, to stop your throat getting dry. It will also come in handy if you are asked any difficult questions - take a long sip of your drink while you come up with a good answer.

- ❤ Don't forget to look the interviewer straight in the eye when you meet them. Shake their hand firmly and smile confidently - that way they'll know how friendly and open you are.

- ❤ Name-dropping can be impressive. Mention your favourite celebrities by their first names to convince the interviewer that you're the best of friends.

- People will soon get bored of hearing about you if you give hundreds of interviews. Only pick your favourite magazine or TV show to talk to and give them an 'exclusive' instead.

- If you're about to appear in your school play or sing in a talent contest bring it up as often as you dare - the more publicity you can get, the better.

- Make sure everyone knows how to spell your name correctly.

How To Be A Supermodel

There's more to being a supermodel than just looking glamorous - it's important to have the attitude too.

- Chew gum, talk on your mobile and demand things.

- Look bored while pretending to read an important work of literature.

- Perfect your 'model walk' - head high, shoulders back, placing one foot directly in front of the other as though you're walking a tightrope.

- Most importantly, never smile.

HOW TO BLOW-DRY YOUR HAIR PERFECTLY

Keep your hair looking sleek and shiny with a salon-style blow-dry at home. This step-by-step guide will help you get it right.

1. Comb your hair gently after shampooing and conditioning to remove any knots. See page 88 if your hair's in a real pickle.

2. Gently squeeze your hair to remove excess water.

3. Wrap your hair up in a towel for five minutes.

4. Get to work with your hairdryer. Make sure you blow-dry down the length of the hair from the roots to the tips – this makes the outer 'cuticle' of each hair lie flat, which means shinier hair.

5. Work the hairdryer quickly over your head, ruffling your hair with your fingers at the same time.

6. Tip your head upside down while you direct the dryer's nozzle at the roots – this will build body into your hair.

7. Only when your hair is just beginning to feel dry, start using a brush to style it – before that, you're wasting your time.

8. Style the front of your hair first – it's the bit that everyone will notice. Work your way around to the sides and back. It may be helpful to use clips to section off parts of the hair you're not working on.

9. Give your hair a final blast of cool air to fix the style.

10. Ruffle with your fingers to add a little texture.

How To Smell Gorgeous

Nothing says glamour like smelling great. Try out these tactics and you'll always be the sweetest-smelling girl around.

Fresh as a Daisy

It goes without saying, but you should have a bath or shower every single day.

Herbal Remedy

Add sprigs of herbs to your bath for a natural treat. Refreshing ones to try are mint, rosemary and thyme – either raid the kitchen cupboard for dried ones or check out the garden for fresh herbs. Once the tub is full, toss in the herbs and let them float in the water to release their scent.

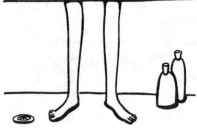

Full Steam Ahead

Adding a few drops of perfume to the floor of the shower will create beautifully scented steam.

A Fresh Start

Sprinkle a dry towel with your favourite fresh fragrance. Put it in the tumble dryer for a few minutes until it heats up and give yourself a vigorous rubdown. The hot fragranced towel will make you feel fabulously awake and alert.

Sweet Dreams

Sprinkle your bedsheets with talcum powder! You'll wake up smelling lovely.

Eat Thai

Smell sweet with Thai food. Believe it or not, this type of food is said to produce the nicest body smells, so take the opportunity to eat lots of it! It contains plenty of aromatic ingredients, such as mint, lemon grass and coconut. Go easy on the garlic, though!

Layers of Loveliness

Learn to layer fragrance to smell beautiful all day. Start with a scented bath oil, and soap. Move on to the body lotion and finish with eau de toilette. Put a perfume gift set on your next birthday or Christmas wish-list.

HOW TO TIE-DYE A T-SHIRT

The best way to brighten up an old white T-shirt is tie-dyeing. It's easier than it looks to create a groovy sunburst design and add some hippy chic to your wardrobe.

What you need:
- A pack of cold-water dye in any colour
- Salt and a metal spoon
- Elastic bands to create the designs
- Rubber gloves to stop the dye staining your hands
- One measuring jug of cold water
- One washing-up bowl of warm water
- One white T-shirt (obviously!).

TOP TIP

Check it's okay to use things from the kitchen beforehand, or buy your own set specially for dyeing.

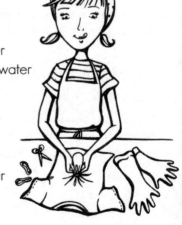

HERE'S HOW:

1. Prepare the mixture – open the dye container and pour the powder into the jug of cold water. Let it dissolve.

2. Add the bag of fixative and the required amount of salt. (Every brand of dye is slightly different, so read the instructions carefully.) Stir until everything's dissolved.

3. Pour the dye mixture into the bowl of warm water. Stir again until thoroughly mixed.

4. To prepare the T-shirt, pinch the fabric in the middle of the front. Securely twist an elastic band around the pinch. The sections of fabric covered by the elastic bands won't absorb the dye and will remain white.

5. Next, bunch the fabric together and tie a second elastic band around the pinch about 5cm from the first.

6. Continue adding elastic bands, 5cm apart, until the front of the T-shirt is completely wrapped.

7. If you like, repeat the same process again on the back of the T-shirt and even on the sleeves.

8. Immerse your T-shirt in the bowl of dye. Push it down into the liquid with the spoon to make sure it's thoroughly wet.

9. Leave your T-shirt to soak for an hour then squeeze out the water and rinse away any excess dye.

10. Hang the T-shirt up on a line to dry, then remove the elastic bands. Voilà, a beautiful sunburst T-shirt.

HOW TO MAKE
A DOOR CURTAIN

C reate a glamorous entrance to your bedroom with a beaded door curtain. It looks fab and is easy to make. Before you start, make sure you ask your parents if it's okay to tack it to your doorframe.

What you need:
- A thick piece of ribbon cut to the same width as your doorframe
- About 30 plastic straws - any colour
- 12 pieces of fishing line or strong clear thread, each 1.8m long
- Plastic beads - around 200.
- A few drawing pins to secure the curtain to your doorframe
- A pair of scissors.

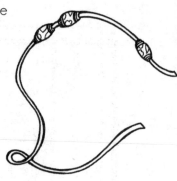

HOW TO MAKE IT:

1. Lay the thick piece of ribbon on the floor. Secure each strand of fishing line to the ribbon at equal intervals - do this by looping one end of the thread over the ribbon and tying a knot.

2. Cut the straws into 5cm lengths.

3. String the beads and straw pieces on to each length of fishing line, alternating them and finishing with a bead.

4. When the fishing line is full, feed the end of the thread through the bead twice – finish with a knot to secure it in place.

5. Repeat for each piece of fishing line.

6. Get an adult to tack the curtain over your door with drawing pins.

How To Lip-Synch Successfully

If you're a pop star who hasn't got a good singing voice, you need to know how to lip-synch. This is miming to look as if you're singing a song when you're not. Here are some tips to help:

- Choose a simple song that you can really put your heart into. Look for one that is funny, emotional or which has a strong beat.

- Learn the lyrics! There's nothing worse than forgetting the words mid-performance.

- Really think about what the words of the song mean and how to express them with your body language.

- ❤ Don't be afraid to exaggerate your facial movements during your performance.

- ❤ Dress up – it will really boost your confidence.

- ❤ Never turn your back on your audience – it will make it more difficult to keep their attention.

- ❤ Don't worry if you think people suspect you're lip-synching – some of the most famous singers do it.

- ❤ If you're not confident enough to perform alone, get a friend or a group of friends to join you. There are plenty of duets and songs by bands to choose from.

How To Clean Your Make-up Brushes

Make-up brushes are the best way to apply make-up but they can get dirty. Wash them regularly to keep your brushes clean and your face healthy.

1. Squirt a little shampoo into a cup and add warm water.

2. Swish the brushes in the water to dissolve dirt, then rinse.

3. Gently squeeze the brushes with your fingers to remove excess moisture.

4. Place a clean towel on a flat surface and lay the brushes on top. Leave them to air-dry.

How To Make A Button And Bead Charm Bracelet

What you need:

- A selection of pretty buttons
- A selection of pretty beads
- Some elastic thread
- Some sewing thread, cut into 10cm lengths.

Ask an adult if you can raid their sewing box for some buttons, snip them off unwanted clothes, or scour sewing stores for bargains.

What To Do:

1. Measure enough elastic to fit around your wrist and then add on 8cm extra. Knot the ends together and snip away any excess.

2. Take one bead or button at a time, and feed a length of sewing thread through its hole. Then secure on the thread with a knot.

3. Now tie the button or bead around the elastic. Secure with a double knot and snip off the excess thread.

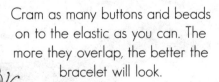

4. Keep on adding buttons and beads until you can't see the elastic any more.

Cram as many buttons and beads on to the elastic as you can. The more they overlap, the better the bracelet will look.

How To Pretend You Can Dance Flamenco

Fool people that you can dance the flamenco with this mini-routine. Get your friends to clap their hands rhythmically while you perform these moves as dramatically as you can.

1. Stand as tall as you can. Reach up with your right arm and pretend you're plucking an apple from a high branch of a tree. Hold the imaginary apple with the very tips of your fingers.

2. Now you must pretend you are going to take a bite from the apple. Rotate your wrist clockwise as you bend your elbow and bring your imaginary apple towards your mouth (don't actually bite).

3. Now start swinging your hips, stomping your feet and turning in circles.

4. Pretend to throw the apple to the ground with a look of utter disgust on your face.

5. Now stamp on the imaginary apple, moving your feet faster and faster as you crush it to a pulp.

6. Repeat.

HOW TO SOOTHE TIRED FEET

It's no surprise that at the end of a hard day at school (or at the shops) your feet can feel tired and sore. Try this quick and simple remedy to bring them back to life.

Start by soaking your feet in a bowl of warm water to which you've added a handful of sea salt. Keep them there for five minutes. Next, try lying down on your back on the floor with your feet up, resting on the edge of the sofa. Stay there for ten minutes.

HOW TO EAT SPAGHETTI LIKE A REAL ITALIAN

Forget about cutting up your spaghetti or fiddling with spoons – all real Italians need is a fork and a little know-how.

1. Poke the prongs of the fork into the spaghetti and scoop up a small amount. Lift it high off the plate to release it from the rest of the spaghetti and to allow any stray strands to fall. If you've taken too much, now's the time to wiggle the fork slightly and let some of the excess fall off.

2. Look for an area of the plate that's food-free. Quickly point the prongs of the fork straight down on to it.

3. Twirl the fork a few times to create a roll of strands.

4. Quickly flick your wrist and place the rolled-up spaghetti into your mouth.

Bravo!

How To Make A Mood Board

The most glamorous girls always know what suits them, as well as the styles and colours they really love. You can work out your own personal style, too, by creating a 'Mood Board' for your bedroom.

First of all, you'll need a pin board for the wall. If you haven't got one of these, try securing four cork floor tiles to your wall with sticky tack.

Now the fun bit ... start collecting clippings from fashion magazines, photos, old postcards, adverts, paint swatches, fabric scraps, leaves - anything at all. The only important thing is that you really love everything. Take your time deciding which things really appeal to you. Spread them out on your bed while you decide. You may be able to gather them into little sections of similar colours or styles.

Once you're happy with your selection, arrange them on to your pin board. Now sit back and take a look - your personal taste will be there for you to admire whenever you want.

How To Walk In High-Heeled Shoes

High-heeled shoes look lovely if you're off to a party or a wedding, but they can be tricky to walk in at first. Follow this simple guide and you'll soon be skipping around like a real lady.

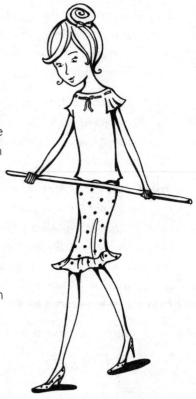

- Choose a low heel or a wedge (where the gap between the heel and toe is filled in) so that you can practise walking more easily – don't aim too high at first.

- Find a good place to practise where you have plenty to hold on to. Stand up slowly and carefully. Your centre of gravity will be higher than usual so flex each knee a little to steady yourself.

- Keep your bottom tucked in and balance on the balls of your feet. Take a few steps placing each heel first before putting your toe down. Be careful not to get a heel caught in the carpet.

- Keep practising at home until you feel ready to go out. Try a short trip around the corner and back before attempting a longer outing. Soon you'll be able to run for a bus with ease.

Take a spare pair of flat shoes along, too, just in case you get tired.

How To Look Beautiful For Free

The best three beauty treats of all are actually free – sleep, fresh air and lots of water.

- Breathing in fresh air oxygenates your skin so that it looks rosy and fresh.

- Drink plenty of water to keep yourself hydrated.

- Sleep gives your body the chance to repair itself so you look even more beautiful the next morning.

How To Seem Confident When You're Not

The next time you're feeling shy and overwhelmed, try out these DOs and DON'Ts to make others think you're feeling completely confident ...

DON'T Wear Dull Colours

Instead of trying to blend in with the background, get yourself noticed by wearing confident reds, oranges or yellows.

DO Get Your Body Language Right

Hold your head high however nervous you feel. Don't clasp your hands in front of you or fold them – it's much better to stand with your arms hanging relaxed and loose at your sides. Sit with your hands resting loosely in your lap.

DON'T Hide Behind Your Hair

Let people see your face – hair swept back into a neat ponytail says that you're okay about people looking at you.

DO Smile

People often confuse shyness with unfriendliness – a smile shows you're friendly and makes people feel relaxed around you.

DON'T Talk Too Quickly

Relax and take a deep breath. Take your time and give yourself a chance to think about what you want to say. Avoid just blurting out the first thing that comes into your head.

DO Look People In The Eye

One of the most obvious signs of shyness is when you avoid making eye contact with the person you're talking to.

DON'T Chew Your Nails

Nibbling on fingers is a dead give-away that you're feeling nervous.

DO Lift Your Spirits With Scent

Apply a dot of grapefruit or bergamot essential oil on your wrists before heading out the door in the morning. They're great for boosting your confidence and you can take a quick sniff whenever you need a lift.

How To Strike A Pose

When everyone is looking your way it's vital to make sure that your every move seems as naturally glamorous as possible, whether you've just popped to the corner shop or you're making a brief appearance at a film premier. Next time you're on the red carpet try out these top moves.

The Hair Flip

As you step on to the school bus smile, wave and flip your head up so that your hair swishes out behind you. Try not to catch yourself in the eye though, as this will sting.

The Look Behind You

Walk past your waiting photographers without stopping. Just when they think you've ignored them completely stop, put one hand on your hip and look back over your shoulder before giving them your best smile.

The Big Tumble

This one is usually best avoided but it's important to be prepared so that you can gracefully jump straight back up again if you fall.

The Good Side

Check yourself out in a mirror to determine which side is your best side.

When in front of the flashing cameras, tilt your head naturally to show off your good side to the photographers.

The Copy Cat

If you have time beforehand, look for posing inspiration in a fashion magazine. Maybe a model or celebrity you admire has a signature pose you really admire. Try to pull it off yourself, but add a twist to make it your own.

Now practise, practise, practise.

How To Look Instantly Taller

G ood posture is the best way to add inches to your height. It'll make you look more confident, too. Look in a mirror and check yourself out.

- ❤ DO keep your neck straight from hairline to shoulders.

- ❤ DON'T let your head hang forward.

- ❤ DO keep your chest high and your shoulder blades flat.

- ❤ DON'T hunch up your shoulders or slump forward.

- ❤ DO stand tall with a shallow curve in the small of your back.

- ❤ DON'T stick your tummy out.

- ❤ DO tuck your bottom in.

- ❤ DON'T stand with your feet turned out – keep them parallel with each other.

How To Emphasize Your Eye Colour

A great way to make your natural eye colour really stand out for parties is to wear clothes in just the right shade. Forget about wearing blues if you have blue eyes, and browns if you have brown eyes – these are the best choices ...

Eye Colour: PALE BLUE
Try: lilac or pastel pink

Eye Colour: MID-TO-DARK BLUE
Try: peach or gold

Eye Colour: LIGHT BROWN
Try: honey brown or khaki green

Eye Colour: DARK BROWN
Try: toffee brown or olive green

Eye Colour: PALE GREEN
Try: lavender or blue-grey

Eye Colour: DARK GREEN
Try: peach or plum

Eye Colour: HAZEL
Try: moss green or purple.

HOW TO FIND THE PERFECT PERFUME

There are thousands of perfumes in the shops, which means it can be hard to whittle them down to find the one you really like and which most suits your personality.

TRIAL AND ERROR

💜 Head for the perfume counter at a department store or a large chemist for the best choice. Try a maximum of three, otherwise your nose will get tired and they will all start to smell the same.

💜 Start by taking a look at the ingredients before you spritz. If you're quite girly you might love floral perfumes. If you're sporty, citrus scents like lemon or grapefruit could be ideal.

💜 Spray a little on the inside of your wrist or elbow, then wait ten minutes for the perfume to 'develop' properly. You shouldn't buy a perfume even if you like it straight away. Perfumes often smell different after a couple of hours. If you like the way it smells on your skin later, you're on to a winner.

Some perfumers recommend spritzing freshly washed hair so that you waft the scent around you as you move your head.

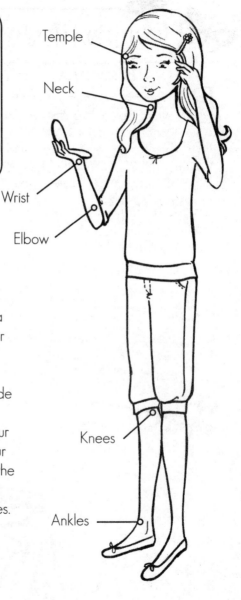

Temple

Neck

Wrist

Elbow

Knees

Ankles

How To Wear It

The best place to wear a perfume is on one of your pulse points - where the blood is closest to your skin's surface. These include your temples, the side of your neck (not behind your ears!), in the crook of your elbow, your inner wrists, the backs of your knees and on the front of your ankles.

How To Bead Your Hair

B eaded hair looks really pretty and costs just pennies. It only takes a little time and practice to achieve.

What you need:

- A handful of beads with large holes. Plastic ones are best as they're lighter - you don't want to be too weighed down.
- A reel of cotton, any colour.

Check out page 131 to see what colour beads will suit your eye colour best.

How To Do It:

1. Pick up a strand of hair about the thickness of a shoelace.

2. Divide it into three smaller strands.

3. Plait the three strands together until you have about 5cm of hair left at the ends.

4. Wet the end of the plait and smooth the ends together.

5. Thread a bead on to the plait and push it up the hair.

6. Add as many beads as you like, carefully pushing each one up the plait.

7. When you've finished, wind a length of cotton around the end of the plait and tie in place. Alternatively, use a thin hairband, if you prefer.

8. Repeat the whole process to make as many plaits as you like. You could even enlist some friends to help you bead all of your hair.

If you want to wear your beautifully beaded hair to school, make sure you check that the school rules allow this first.

How To Look After Your Skin In Summer

Everyone loves a day at the beach in summer - but no one likes getting burnt by the sun. Check out this safe tan plan.

- 💜 Apply suntan lotion (SPF 15 or higher) first thing in the morning before getting dressed - that way you won't miss any areas.

- 💜 Lips are especially prone to burning and chapping in the sun - so slick on some lip salve.

- 💜 Stay out of the sun between 12 noon and 3 o'clock when the sun is at its hottest. Move into the shade or cover up with a T-shirt and a broad-brimmed hat.

- 💜 If you're a sporty type or fancy a cooling dip in the sea, choose a special waterproof sun lotion.

How To Look After Your Skin In Winter

❤ Chilly temperatures and cold winds can make your skin dry and itchy. Always protect yourself with warm mittens, cosy scarves and cute hats.

❤ Dress in layers that will keep you warm from top to toe. Light cotton next to the skin helps keep your skin warm and dry.

❤ Bathe or shower in lukewarm water. Hot baths may sound nice but the heat can dry out the natural oils in your skin making it even itchier than before.

❤ Don't lick sore lips to try and soothe them, you'll make them even flakier. Slick on some balm or petroleum jelly instead.

How To Take Charge Of Out-Of-Control Hair

The weather can wreak havoc on your hair. If your pretty curls have a case of the frizzies, or fly-away static is ruining your lovely tresses, try these helpful hints to take control of your locks.

Fly-Away

- The dry winter air can literally make your hair stand on end. Use a wooden brush and this will help to reduce static electricity.

- Use a moisturising shampoo and conditioner to stop your hair drying out.

- Spritz anti-static hairspray on to your brush before styling your hair.

FRIZZY

- ❤ Use a conditioner each time you wash your hair to keep it as sleek as possible – save lots of time with a spray-on and leave-in brand.

- ❤ Use your fingers as styling tools instead of brushes and combs – you're less likely to create frizz.

- ❤ Rub a few drops of almond oil between your palms, then smooth over your hair to combat crazy curls.

How To Choose The Right Sunglasses For Your Face Shape

Choosing the right pair of shades to suit your face shape can transform your whole look and give you just the right finishing touch. Check out how to work out your face shape on page 46, then decide which frames would suit you the best.

Round-Shaped Face

Look for broad styles which are equal to the width of your face. Square lenses look good, too.

Heart-Shaped Face

Delicate or rimless frames suit your pretty face shape perfectly. Angular shapes are also a good choice for you.

Square-Shaped Face

Soft, gently curved, oval-shaped frames soften your defined features perfectly.

Oval-Shaped Face

Lucky thing – everything suits you!

HOW TO BE
A GODDESS

O wing to the goddess-like status you have now achieved by reading this book, you'll need to learn how to cope with the stresses and strains this role may bring.

💜 If you really want to look like a goddess then borrow an old, white sheet and drape it around yourself in the style of a Roman toga.

💜 Wind some pretty flowers through your hair and always remember to leave a trail of blossoms wherever you walk.

💜 Smile gently at all times to give people the impression that you're calm and serene.

💜 If people are nice enough to offer you gifts, do your best to accept them with good manners (even if you'd rather they hadn't bothered).

💜 One of the best goddess skills you will learn is wisdom. Use it well and try to give the best advice you can.

💜 Most importantly – never abuse your powers.

How To Be Fabulous With Money

Wouldn't it be fabulous if you had enough money to buy everything you ever wanted? Unfortunately, that just isn't possible. The more money you have, the more you want, but follow these top tips and you can make your pocket money go further.

Look After The Pennies

It's important to keep track of your money – how much you have and how much you're planning to spend. Here are some top money-saving tips.

- It is much easier to save when you have a goal in mind. Make a list of all the things you want to buy and how much they cost. Then work out how long it will take you to save your pocket money for them.

- Be realistic. Cross off anything on the list that you don't really need or that you can make yourself. This way you will get your hands on the things you really want sooner.

- Every penny counts. Leave your purse at home when you don't need it. Every magazine or hair clip you buy eats into your savings and leaves you further away from your prize.

GET YOUR HANDS DIRTY

Grown-ups have to go to work to make a living and, even though going to school can sometimes be a chore, it isn't quite the same thing. You need to show your parents that you are prepared to work hard for extra money. Let them know what you are saving for and ask if there is anything you can do to help around the house or garden. Hopefully, they will admire your responsible attitude and reward your labours with some extra cash.

MAKE DO AND MEND

Try jazzing up some old things you have. You will be surprised at how much you already have lying around at home that can be transformed into something fabulous.

- ❤ Instead of buying a new outfit, use scarves, belts or jewellery to update an old one.

- ❤ Making gifts for friends and family is a great way to save pennies – and handmade things are always extra special.

HOW TO WIN A TALENT CONTEST

Winning a talent show takes ambition, courage and, of course, a talent that sets you apart from the other competitors. The key to winning often lies in impressing the audience rather than the judges. If the judges can see that the audience think you're fabulous, they are more likely to award you mega-points. Here's a handy guide to wowing the crowd.

If your school does not run a talent contest, why not suggest the idea to your teacher?

Top Talent Tips

- ❤ You're probably a multi-talented lady, but focus on one talent and stick to it. Someone juggling with fire while singing and baking cupcakes is less likely to impress than someone doing one thing really, really well.

- ❤ Whatever it is you're doing, you want the audience to enjoy it. Having a big grin on your face is a sure way to get them in the mood. Practise your facial expressions in front of a mirror, so that you look relaxed and smiley, even if you're concentrating very hard.

- ❤ You want your performance to have the 'wow' factor, so take time to prepare your look. You could wear something dazzling and sparkly, be lit by a single, blinding spotlight, or ask some friends to help by becoming your fabulous backing dancers.

- ❤ Try not to take yourself too seriously. If you strut around acting as if you are the best thing ever, don't be surprised if people find it off-putting and don't vote for you. It is great to be confident, but don't be arrogant.

- ❤ Try to resist bursting out laughing or teasing other contestants when they slip up or have a mishap - however tempting it may be. Be a good friend and calm other people's nerves.

How To Ride Out Embarrassing Moments

Whether it is calling your teacher 'Mum', or falling over in front of your crush, embarrassing things happen to everyone from time to time. Follow the tips below to make sure you know how to deal with even the most cringe-worthy situations with style.

Damage Control

After an embarrassing accident has happened, take a look around. Has anyone actually noticed? You may have been lucky and got away with it. People are often too busy thinking about how cool they are to notice your mistakes. If no one draws attention to your slip, move on. There is no need to point it out yourself.

Laugh It Off

If your mistake was too obvious for anyone to miss – such as falling over during a school play or taking a tumble halfway down the catwalk – get up quickly and smile. People will love you for this. You may want the ground to open up and swallow you whole, or to start a new life in another country, but the less embarrassed you show people you are, the less likely they are to tease you about it. If you appear not to be bothered, why should they be?

STAY COOL

Stay calm. This will help you to avoid going red in the face. Develop the ability to brush off embarrassment like water off a duck's back. Getting upset will only draw more attention to yourself. Don't stick around and allow a crowd to gather around you. Leave the scene of your crime with a good friend, as soon as you can. You will soon be laughing about it.

STAY IN PERSPECTIVE

Cringe-worthy things happen even to the most fabulous of people. You may feel bad for a while and people may even tease you, but this will pass. Try not to get too upset over it. The more dramatic you are, the more you will remind people about what has happened.

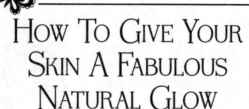

How To Give Your Skin A Fabulous Natural Glow

Forget expensive cosmetics – your young skin has a natural glow that no beauty lotion or potion can copy. Follow these simple rules and make the most of the youthful radiance that all grown-ups long for.

Don't Wash It Down The Plughole

As tempting as it is, don't stay too long in a hot bath or shower. While you might think steaming-hot showers are good for you, they actually draw the moisture out of your skin, and skin needs to retain its moisture to look its best.

Catch Some Zzzzzzzzs

Getting enough sleep is a must. Your body repairs itself during sleep, so avoid too many late nights. This way your skin will look fresh and radiant, and you'll have bag-free eyes, too!

Get Sweaty

Exercising is not just good for a healthy body, but perfect for great-looking skin, too. Sweating is your body's natural way of eliminating nasty impurities that can clog up the pores of your skin, causing spots and pimples. So what are you waiting for?

Food, Fabulous Food

Eating foods rich in vitamins helps skin to look its best. Make sure you eat plenty of tomatoes, sweet potatoes, cantaloupe melon, citrus fruit, spinach and broccoli. If you can eat oily fish once or twice a week, such as salmon or tuna, this will also give your skin a natural boost.

Some scientists believe that garlic in your diet helps to improve the life span of your skin cells. So ask your parents to cook with it a few times a week.

How To Banish Boredom Forever

O nly boring people get bored. Grown-ups love saying this, but funnily enough it is true. Fill your free time with fun activities, and you will find that you never need to hear those infuriating five words again.

Change Your Attitude

The first thing to do is adopt a 'P.M.A.' – meaning a 'Positive Mental Attitude'. Look at free time as a fabulous opportunity to do something fun and enjoy some quality 'you' time.

Get Up

Don't laze around in bed or on the sofa. Sitting around doing nothing will only make you feel miserable and even more bored.

Get Moving

As soon as you start to feel bored, try and do some exercise. Exercise is a great way to lift your spirits and get yourself in the mood to find something fabulous to do. Why not create your own dance routine in your room or learn how to twirl a baton? If you don't want to do something that adventurous, take a brisk walk around the park for some fresh air.

GET FABULOUS

Take this free time as an opportunity to make yourself even more fabulous than you already are. Reading and listening to new music are great ways to relax and pass the time and will give you something interesting to talk about the next time you see your friends.

COUNTING THE DAYS

Check your calendar to see if there are any friends' birthdays coming up – you may need to make a birthday card or present for them. Home-made gifts are so much more personal. If you have time, you could even make yourself a little something.

CALL FOR HELP

Do you feel sociable? Maybe you could call a few friends to see if they want some company, too. Make sure you ask your parents before you use the phone.

HOW TO TURN YOUR BEDROOM INTO A HAVEN

*Y*our bedroom says a lot about you, so you want to make sure you are sending out the right message to any visitors. Follow these top tips so that anyone who sees your bedroom will be in no doubt whatsoever that it belongs to a truly fabulous girl.

GET THINGS STRAIGHT

Your room needs to be a haven for you to escape to, not a pit you want to escape from. Getting things looking neat and tidy will create the illusion of space and make your room seem much larger than it is.

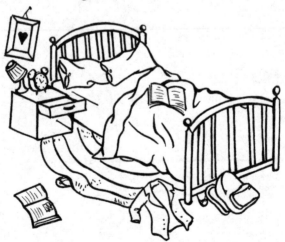

TRASH IT

Trash unwanted stuff, not your room, that is. Be brutal with items you no longer need - either throw them out or ask an adult to drop them off at a charity shop. The fewer things you have, the fewer things you have to tidy.

HAVE A PLACE FOR EVERYTHING

Don't just throw your things on the floor when you get in. Give all of your things a home and put them in the same place every day.

TRAIN YOURSELF TO BE TIDY

Train yourself to be tidy by developing a routine. Always make your bed and open your curtains before you leave for school. Pile clean clothes on your bed so that you will have to put them away before you can get into bed at night.

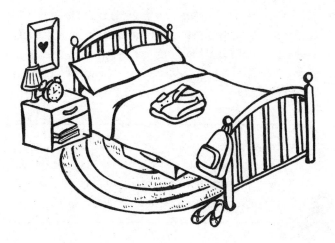

How To Add Glamour To Your Bedroom

These simple touches will add a fresh and funky feel to your room.

❤ Tie back your curtains with wide, coloured ribbons so that they frame your windows nicely. Choose ribbon that goes with the colours already in your room, or make a bold statement and go for bright, contrasting shades.

❤ Hang a string of fairy lights over your bed to make a canopy any princess would be proud of. You'll be sure to feel relaxed, surrounded by twinkling lights.

❤ Add that personal touch by putting up a few pictures. Choose either photographs of your friends and family or your favourite place or animal, or just pictures you like from a magazine. Simply pop them into old picture frames and hang them on your wall.

If your room feels a little on the small side, hang a large mirror opposite your window. The mirror will double the amount of light in your room during the daytime, making it feel much bigger.

❤ To add a splash of colour to your desk or dressing table, nothing beats a bouquet of flowers. Fresh flowers are best, but if you don't have any, use silk flowers instead. Choose blooms that reflect your style - go cute and girly with roses and lilies, or bold and quirky with bright sunflowers, tulips or orchids.

How To Look Fabulous For P.E.

L ooking good should always be at the top of every glamorous girl's agenda, even during P.E. You want to look your best for the cameras when you score the winning goal, don't you?

Sort Your Hair

Firstly, you need to keep your hair away from your face. If you have long hair, a neat mid to high ponytail will create a really sporty image. If you have shorter hair, an elasticated hair band or Alice band will also give the illusion that you mean business on the pitch.

Face Facts

A clean face (that means one without make-up) is always best for sports. It's fine to wear some tinted lip balm, but leave it at that.

KIT COOLNESS

You don't need to deviate from the school kit to look good. Looking cool is all about attitude. School uniform is a fact of life, so be cool enough to accept it. That way you'll ooze confidence rather than looking like you're trying too hard.

Keep your kit clean and fresh by taking it home once a week to be washed.

HOW TO BE A STYLIST TO THE STARS

Celebrities may get all the attention when it comes to looking fabulous, but where would they be without their equally-fabulous stylists? Here's how to rule the stylist world.

- ♥ Attend all the top fashion shows to find out the latest looks.

- ♥ Select a stunning outfit for your star to wear.

- ♥ Chew gum and talk loudly on your mobile phone.

- ♥ Wear huge sunglasses while you dress your star.

How To Make A Fabulous Foaming Buff-Puff

This pretty puff can either be the perfect present for a gal pal or a great way to treat yourself to super-soft skin.

What you need:
- 1m of soft tulle netting in a pretty colour (available from your local fabric shop)
- A needle with a large eye
- Some thread in a matching colour to the tulle
- ½m of ribbon
- Some pins.

1. Spread the tulle out flat in front of you. Fold it over 10cm up from the bottom edge. Fold over again and again until all the fabric has been folded into a tube that is 10cm wide.

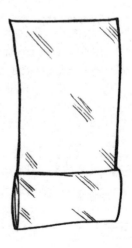

2. Secure the tube of fabric with pins. Sew all the way down the centre of the tube from one end to the other using a simple back stitch. Secure your stitches by sewing repeatedly in the same spot and then tying a knot in your thread.

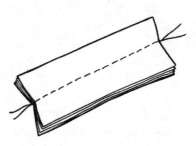

3. Cut carefully along each folded edge of your tulle tube, then cut another piece of thread, roughly twice as long as the tube. Make a knot at the end of the thread and, using loose stitches, sew along the centre of the tulle again.

4. Instead of securing your stitches when you reach the end, remove your needle and pull on the thread, so that the tulle gathers into a pretty puff.

5. Fold the puff into a loop and stitch the ends together. Tie a knot in your thread to secure your stitches. Thread your ribbon through the loop of the puff and tie it into a pretty bow. Fabulous!

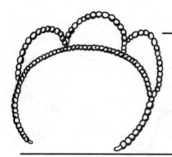

How To Make A Tiara Fit For A Princess

This easy-to-make tiara is perfect for parties, or if you fancy looking utterly fabulous just for the fun of it.

What you need:
- 2 pipe cleaners 30cm long
- Lots of beads with holes wide enough to fit over two pipe cleaners.

What To Do:

1. Take the two pipe cleaners and fix them together by pushing one end of each through a single bead. Push the bead along the pipe cleaners until it is about 5cm away from the ends.

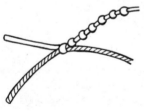

2. Thread more beads on to the longer end of one of your pipe cleaners, until you have a beaded branch about 6cm long. This will form the bottom strand of your tiara. Thread more beads on the other pipe cleaner, this time adding a couple extra to make this branch slightly longer than the first. This branch will form the top of your tiara.

3. Bend the top pipe cleaner over into an arch shape. Bring the two pipe cleaners together by sliding a bead over both ends and pushing it along until it meets the bottom of the beaded branches, forming a loop.

4. Repeat step **2**, this time making two branches about 8cm long. Add a couple more beads to the top branch as you did before. Bring the pipe cleaners together with a bead to make another loop.

5. Repeat steps **2** and **3** again to form another 6cm loop, just like the first one you made.

6. Bring both pipe cleaners together and thread more beads over both so that they form one strand. Keep threading with beads until you reach 1cm before the ends. Repeat this for the other two loose ends. Secure your final beads by folding the ends of the pipe cleaners over.

7. Shape your tiara by bending it into the arch shape of an Alice band. Tweak the loops so that they stand up. Perfect. Now simply pop the tiara on top of your head and find the nearest ball or party.

How To Make Your Own Designer Wellies

Now you can make a splash in style with a glamorous pair of designer Wellington boots. You can guarantee no one will have a pair quite like yours.

What you need:
- A pair of plain Wellingtons
- A bowl of hot soapy water
- A piece of paper
- A pencil
- A felt-tip pen
- Some acrylic paints
- A paintbrush.

What To Do:

1. Before you start, make sure your Wellingtons are completely clean. Wash them in a bowl of hot, soapy water, then rinse them with clean water and leave them to dry.

2. Take a piece of paper and a pencil and sketch out a design for your Wellingtons. Choose simple shapes that you can repeat – rainbows or raindrops will look great, or some flashy bolts of lightning. Alternatively, you could attempt to brighten up a dull day by choosing some funky summer flowers.

3. When you are happy with your design and your Wellingtons are completely dry, use your felt-tip pen to draw your design on to your boots. Don't worry if you make a mistake, you can always paint over it later.

4. Fill in the outlines of the shapes using acrylic paints. Choose bright colours to make your design stand out. Leave your boots to dry.

Now all you need to do is wait for the rain to start falling and jump into the biggest puddle you can find.

> Acrylic paints are waterproof, so your designs will stay bright no matter how muddy the puddles. If the paint begins to chip or flake, wash your boots again and touch up your design with some fresh paint.

HOW TO GET VIP TREATMENT FOR FREE

Sometimes it seems that rich, famous and glamorous people are given everything for free. And they can afford to buy things! Well, now that you are glamorous, the same applies to you.

THE SWEET SMELL OF SUCCESS

Beauty counters in department stores are usually happy to give away free samples of perfumes and skin treatments (as long as you ask politely and don't go back every week for more). Pluck up the courage to ask. After all, you're not doing anything wrong, and you are a future customer. Save your sweet-smelling samples and skin creams to wear on special occasions. If you are feeling extra brave, you could even ask an assistant to give you a free make-over.

A Taste Of The High Life

Believe it or not the supermarket is a great place for freebies, too. The delicatessen counter often has a selection of tasty treats for hungry shoppers to try. If you can't see anything on the counter, hang around for a while. The sales assistants are sure to offer you something if you are polite when they ask if you need any help.

The same goes for the ice-cream bar. Before you order, have a good look at all the flavours available. Ask if you can try any of the unusual ones first. Lots of ice-cream bars encourage this, as they want you to buy more ice cream.

WARNING: Don't try this if the counters in shops look busy. Shop assistants are far less likely to help you, and you will annoy other customers.

Happy Birthday To You ...

Letting a restaurant know that it is either your birthday or the birthday of one of your friends is guaranteed to get you the star treatment when you are out for dinner. Tell one of the waiters whose special day it is and wait to see what happens.

WARNING: Telling someone it is your birthday can be embarrassing, because it may mean you will have to stand on your chair while the whole restaurant sings to you. Decide whether you think this is worthwhile for a free bit of cake.

HOW TO HAVE
A FABULOUS FLIGHT

B egin and end your holiday in style by following these top tips for looking 'plane' perfect when you are jetting off.

BEFORE TAKE OFF

- 💜 Wear loose-fitting clothes, with a few layers on your top half. The temperature on board a flight can go up and down. This way you can stay as cool or keep as warm as you need.

- 💜 Pack a clean top in your hand luggage. Turbulence and bad weather can make eating and drinking tricky, and arriving at your destination in dirty clothes is a definite no-no.

- 💜 Put long hair back in a neat plait to keep it out of your face. Avoid ponytails as these can make leaning back in your seat uncomfortable.

IN FLIGHT

- 💜 Flying can dry out your skin. Pack a tiny pot of moisturizer or aftersun and some lip balm in your hand luggage. Apply your lip balm and moisturizer at least once every two hours – this will stop your skin from drying out.

♥ To stop you from feeling high and dry, make sure you drink plenty of water. Avoid fizzy drinks, as these can dry you out even more.

♥ Sitting still for a long time can cause fluid to build up in your legs and ankles, which makes them swell up. To stop this, get up and move around the cabin as much as you can. When this isn't possible, try these simple exercises in your seat:

ANKLE CIRCLES: Remove your shoes and imagine you are trying to draw a circle with your big toe. Circle your ankle clockwise and then anti-clockwise. Repeat this ten times with each leg.

KNEE LIFTS: Lift your right knee to your chest and then let it drop. Lift your left knee and let it drop. Repeat this ten times.

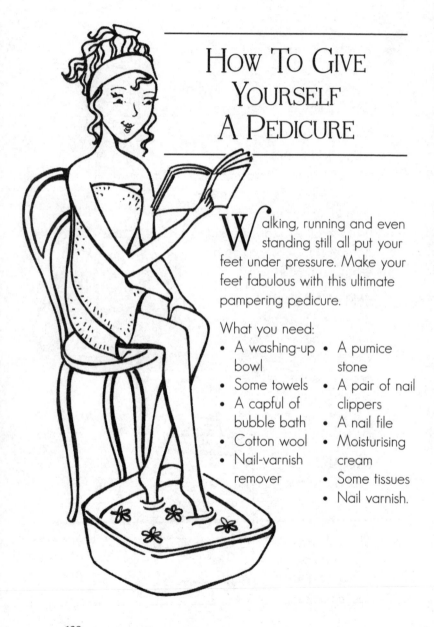

How To Give Yourself A Pedicure

Walking, running and even standing still all put your feet under pressure. Make your feet fabulous with this ultimate pampering pedicure.

What you need:
- A washing-up bowl
- Some towels
- A capful of bubble bath
- Cotton wool
- Nail-varnish remover
- A pumice stone
- A pair of nail clippers
- A nail file
- Moisturising cream
- Some tissues
- Nail varnish.

1. First remove any old nail varnish. Soak a ball of cotton wool in a little nail-polish remover and sweep this over your nails until they are polish-free. Never pick off old varnish, as this can damage the surface of your nails.

2. Lay a towel on the floor in front of a comfortable chair and half fill a washing-up bowl with warm water and some bubble bath. Carry the bowl carefully and place the bowl on the towel. Take a seat and soak your feet in the bowl for ten minutes. Then pat your feet dry with a towel.

3. Take your nail clippers and cut your toenails straight across the tips. Don't try and cut them in one snip but gently take off bits of nail with the clippers. Always leave an area of white at the top of the nail, this will ensure you haven't cut them too short.

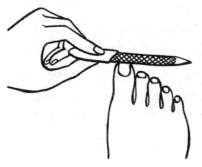

4. Tidy up your trimmed toenails using a nail file. Gently sweep the flat edge of the file across the tops of your nails to smooth down any rough edges.

5. Take a look at your soaked feet. If patches of skin on your heels feel rough and you can scrape some off with your fingernail, this is dead skin. Remove it by rubbing gently with the pumice stone. Don't rub too hard, as young feet don't have much hard, dead skin on them.

6. Once you're happy that your feet feel baby-soft, rinse your feet with clean water and dry them with a towel.

7. Apply a generous amount of moisturizer or, if you have some, foot cream. Let this soak in while you choose a shade of nail varnish.

8. Before you start painting your nails, separate your toes with a folded tissue. Take the tissue and fold it over and over again lengthways until you have a band about 2cm wide. Thread it between your toes. This will stop your toes moving and messing up your varnish.
If you want to glam up your toenails for the summer, why not paint a pretty flower on each nail? (See page 79.)

9. Wipe the surface of your nails with a tissue to remove any moisturizer. Take your nail varnish and apply the first coat. Leave it to dry before applying a second coat. Wait at least 30 minutes before putting on your most glamorous flip-flops.

How To Beat The Blues

Try one of these simple ideas to cheer yourself up the next time you're feeling a little down.

❤ Phone your best friend for a cheerful chat.

❤ Plan a great day out or weekend treat. You will really look forward to it.

❤ Watch your favourite funny movie.

❤ Keep a memory box full of 'happy things'. A good rummage through old birthday cards, invitations and favourite photographs will clear the clouds.

❤ Put on your favourite music and dance away the blues.

> If you find yourself feeling especially gloomy for a long time, don't be afraid to talk to your parents about how you're feeling.

How To Walk Your Dog With Style

G etting out into the great outdoors should never be a chore. Going on a brisk walk is fabulous exercise and will brighten your skin. Don't worry if you don't have a dog - follow these tips to look your best on a walk in the park or a day out in the country.

Looking The Part

Style is important, but wearing your favourite party shoes, no matter how fabulous they are, is not recommended. You might look a bit silly, and you could even end up spoiling them or toppling over in the mud. So, before you leave the house, choose from these three fabulous looks:

Sporty Sister

Put on a clean pair of tracksuit bottoms, a stylish T-shirt and some trainers. Top off the look with a cool baseball cap and a cute ponytail.

Urban Cool

Team your favourite pair of jeans with a pair of walking shoes and a body warmer. Complete the look with a delicious take-away hot chocolate and a magazine.

Country Lady

Tuck your jeans into your Wellington boots and pop on a hat or a headscarf to protect your hair from the wind.

How To Be The Coolest Party Guest

- ❤ Always be fashionably late – 20 minutes or so is ideal.

- ❤ Smile and look around at everyone when you enter a room – people will want to come and talk to you.

- ❤ Mingle with as many people as possible. Next time people will notice if you're not there and you'll probably end up with even more party invitations.

HOW TO HAVE
A FABULOUS
CASCADE OF CURLS

Styling your hair into curls couldn't be simpler and is guaranteed to give you a Hollywood-starlet look. Follow these simple steps with long hair for show-stopping style.

What you need:
- An old sheet or large offcut of fabric
- A ruler
- A pair of scissors
- A hair band.

1. Cut your sheet or fabric into lots of strips, each measuring about 5cm wide by 20cm long.

2. Wash and condition your hair, then comb it through while it is still damp until there are no tangles.

3. Separate your hair into two parts, by twisting the top half of your hair into a looped topknot as shown. Secure this with a hair band.

4. Take a section of the hair that is still loose. It should be a couple of centimetres thick. Comb it through again.

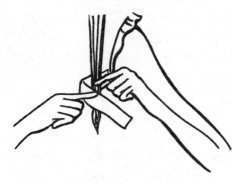

5. Take one of your fabric strips and fold it in half around the bottom of the section of hair, as shown here.

6. Roll the section of hair up the strip, so that the hair wraps around the width of the fabric. Try to wrap the hair around the strip tightly - the tighter you wrap, the bouncier your curls will be. Once you have reached your head, secure the strip by tying the two ends in a knot.

7. Repeat this technique, rolling small sections of hair, until the bottom part of your hair is all in rolls.

8. Now let down the top part of your hair and comb it through. Separate small sections of hair a couple of centimetres wide and repeat steps **5** and **6** until the top part of your hair is all in rolls.

9. Leave your hair to dry. For best results leave it rolled up overnight. This might be a bit uncomfortable, but the results will be worth waiting for.

Top Tip

If you really don't want to sleep with your hair rolled up, dry it with a hairdryer on its coolest setting.

Letting Your Hair Down

10. Once your hair has dried completely, it is time to remove your fabric strips. Undo the knot in each strip and carefully unravel your hair from it.

11. Continue to unravel all of the strips. Avoid running your fingers through the curls at this stage. They are much easier to manage while they are still tightly wound.

12. Put all of your fabric strips to one side to use again.

13. Style your hair by teasing the curls apart using your fingertips. If any of them are sticking out awkwardly, calm them down by spreading on a little water with the palms of your hands. You should now have a headful of perfect curls. Gorgeous - and they will look even more fabulous tomorrow after you have slept on them for one night.

> For super-glossy curls, spritz your hair with a leave-in conditioner while it is still damp and before you roll it in the strips.

HOW TO APPEAR COSMOPOLITAN

To be 'cosmopolitan' means that you are a stylish lady who has seen the world. However, you don't have to jump on an aeroplane to make people think that you're a sophisticated jet-setter. Simply sprinkle your speech with some fabulous foreign expressions to add some 'va-va-voom' to your vocabulary.

VOILÀ

Pronounced: *Vwa la*
In French means: 'There it is'. Use it when you have completed a project, or a set of instructions for someone, or even when you're passing an item to a friend.

C'est La Vie

Pronounced: *Say la vee*
In French means: 'That's life'.
Use it when something hasn't gone exactly to plan.
Sigh deeply and shrug your shoulders when you say
it, for added effect.

Ciao

Pronounced: *Chow*
In Italian means: 'Hello' or 'Goodbye'.
If you're saying it to a girl friend, add 'Bella', which means
'Beautiful', on the end of it to sound even more authentic.

Prego

Pronounced: *Pray-go*
In Italian means: 'You're welcome'.
Say it straight away after anyone thanks you.

Hasta Mañana

Pronounced: *Asta manyana*
In Spanish means: 'See you tomorrow'.
Say it breezily as you leave school.

To add a cosmopolitan edge to
saying 'Hello', greet your friends
with an 'air kiss' on each cheek
(see page 13).

How To Turn An Old Pair Of Jeans Into A Fab Skirt

Here's the perfect way to recycle an old pair of jeans you don't like and turn them into a skirt you'll love.

What you need:
- An old pair of jeans
- A pair of scissors
- Some thread
- A needle – strong enough to get through denim
- Pretty cotton fabric (optional).

HERE'S HOW:

1. Take the pair of jeans and cut straight across both legs at the length you would like your skirt to be.

2. Cut carefully up the inside seam of each leg and trim off the extra fabric. At the front, cut to just below the fly and overlap the curved sections. At the back, cut to about 5cm below the waist band.

3. On a flat surface overlap the curved sections at the front and back and sew into place.

4. From one of the pieces of cast-off legs, cut a triangle large enough to fill the gap between the legs (alternatively, you could use a pretty cotton fabric to contrast with the denim).

5. Either sew the triangles to the insides of the legs by hand or use a sewing machine.

6. Don't bother hemming the bottom of the skirt if you want to wear it straight away - the frayed look is very cool.

If you're feeling creative sew a length of ribbon or lace trimming around the hem to add an extra touch of glamour.

How To Make Afternoon Tea

What better way to spend a summer afternoon than by enjoying delicious dainty treats with your most fabulous friends?

> If the weather is good enough, you could host your afternoon tea outside in the sunshine.

Laying The Table

Spread the table with a pretty tablecloth. A white one with flowers is best if you have one. If you don't, simply cover the table with a plain white bedsheet. Lay the table with a small side plate for each guest. Afternoon tea is a dainty affair, so dinner plates should only be used as serving plates in the centre of the table and not for eating from.

Treats To Eat

Afternoon tea is more of a snack than a full meal, so make sure your treats are beautifully bite-sized. Sandwiches should be cut into dainty fingers rather than triangles, and crusts should be removed. Follow the easy recipes on the next pages to make your afternoon tea the toast of the town.

Say It With Flowers

Nothing makes a table look lovelier than a simple arrangement of fresh flowers in the centre of the table. They needn't be anything fancy, just a few sweet peas from the garden or even some dandelions and daisies arranged in a vase or water glass – something to give the feeling of bringing the outdoors in.

Fantastic Finger Sandwiches

What you need:
- 4 slices of brown bread
- 4 slices of white bread
- 2 slices of ham
- Cream cheese
- Thin slices of cucumber.

1. Take four slices of brown bread, and spread one side of each slice with cream cheese.

2. Cover two slices of the bread with slices of cucumber and then sprinkle with a little salt and pepper.

3. Cover the cucumber layer with the two spare slices of brown bread, cream-cheese side down, just as you would with a normal sandwich, and press them down.

4. Use a table knife to trim off all of the crusts, and then cut your sandwiches into three equal fingers. You should have six sandwiches all together.

5. Repeat this with the white bread, but this time use the slices of ham instead of cucumber.

DELICIOUS ICED TEA

What you need:

- 4 tea bags
- 500ml boiling water
- 1 litre cold water
- 225 g caster sugar
- 2 lemons cut in half
- Lots of ice.

1. Place the tea bags into a heat-proof measuring jug. Pour in the boiling water. Ask an adult to help you with this.

2. Stir the tea bags and water together for about 1 minute. Leave the tea bags in the water for 30 minutes.

3. After 30 minutes, remove the tea bags.

4. Stir in the sugar until it is all dissolved.

5. Pour the sweet tea into a jug that is big enough to hold the rest of the water and ice. Add the cold water and squeeze in the juice from your lemons.

6. Give your tea a good stir and add the ice.

7. Pour into tall glasses and enjoy.

> If your parents have some pretty crockery and glasses, ask if you can use these for your treats.

How To Make A Fabulous Cake Stand

B righten up your birthday table with this gorgeous, easy-to-make cake stand. Pile it high with the most superb sweet or savoury snacks, for the prettiest way to present your party food.

What you need:
- 3 pretty party cups (paper or plastic)
- A sharp pencil
- A blob of modelling clay
- 3 m of gift ribbon
- 2 small pretty party plates
- 1 large pretty party plate
- A pair of Scissors
- Some sticky tape.

1. Place one of your cups on top of a ball of modelling clay. Make a hole in the bottom of the cup by pushing a sharp pencil through the centre into the clay. Repeat this with the other cups and the three plates.

2. Fold the ribbon in half and cut it into two equal lengths. Hold the pieces of ribbon together and thread them through the hole in one of the cups. Pull them through.

3. Thread the ribbons through the other cups and plates in the following order: through the top of a small plate; through the bottom of the second cup; through the top of the other small plate, and then through the bottom of the last cup.

4. Finally, thread the ribbons through the top of the large plate. Secure the ends of the ribbon to the bottom of the final plate with sticky tape, so that they can't slip back through.

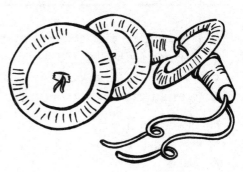

5. Take hold of the loose ends of the ribbon on the first cup and sit the cake stand on its base. Bring the cake stand together by pulling on the ribbons and tying the two ends in a knot and then a pretty bow.

6. Curl the ends of the ribbon by holding them flat against the blade of your scissors at the base of your bow. Scrape the scissors down the length of the ribbon. Let the curls cascade down the tiers of the stand, then load it with your favourite treats.

How To Make A New-York-Style Brunch

B runch is the perfect treat for fabulous friends who are feeling peckish after a sleepover. It is the equivalent of a late breakfast or an early lunch, so your guests should be up, dressed and ready for the day.

What you need:
(to serve four)
- 4 bagels, cut in half
- 6 eggs
- 50ml of milk
- Salt and pepper
- A knob of butter
- 4 slices of ham or smoked salmon.

1. Crack your eggs into a jug by tapping each one against the rim of the jug until it breaks open and then pull the shells apart. Remove any pieces of shell that fall into the jug.

2. Beat the eggs using a fork until all the yolks are broken and you can't see any of the clear white. Add salt and pepper and stir in the milk. Put the jug to one side.

3. Toast your bagels in the toaster one at a time and keep them warm in the oven, set to a low heat.

4. Melt the butter in a saucepan over a medium heat. Ask an adult to help you with this.

5. When the butter has melted, pour in the eggs and stir with a wooden spoon. The eggs will begin to cook and set, so keep stirring to stop them sticking to the bottom of the pan.

6. When your eggs are all light and fluffy and there is no runny egg left in the pan, remove them from the heat.

7. Take your bagels out of the oven, and place the bottom half of each one on a plate. Spoon a quarter of your eggs on to each bagel.

8. Place a slice of ham or smoked salmon on top of the eggs, and then pop the top on to each of the bagels. Serve with a cool glass of orange juice.

How To Make
A Fabulous Birdbath

B irds love to have a good bath – somewhere clean and safe where they can preen their feathers and have a drink. Keep the birds in your garden looking their best with an easy-to-make birdbath – the perfect place for feathered friends to freshen up after a long flight.

What you need:
- 3 terracotta plant pots in 3 different sizes
- A terracotta plant tray
- A handful of gravel and some stones
- Some water.

1. Choose a spot out in the open for your birdbath, so that your feathered friends have a good view of any pesky cats approaching.

2. Make the pedestal of the birdbath. Turn the largest plant pot upside down and place the next-smallest pot on top of it so that it fits snugly over the bottom of the pot below.

3. Now turn the smallest pot upside down and fit this over the bottom of the medium-sized pot.

4. Take your plant tray and sit this on top of the smallest pot to make the bath for your birds to splash about in.

Don't be tempted to paint the birdbath in bright colours as this will discourage birds from using it.

5. Place a couple of handfuls of gravel and some stones in the bottom of your tray. This will help any small creatures that find their way inside the tray to climb out again. It will also make the base of the bath less slippery for the birds.

6. Now all you need to do is fill the birdbath with some water from the tap and wait for the birds to discover their new oasis. Keep a bird book handy so you can identify them as they fly in to spruce themselves up.

7. Don't forget to check your birdbath regularly to make sure the water is clean and fresh. The rain should keep it topped up, but if you see it is dry add some water.

WARNING: Take your birdbath apart when there is bad weather as it could fall over and break.

ALSO AVAILABLE ...

The Girls' Book 1: How To
Be The Best At Everything
ISBN: 978-1-905158-79-9

The Girls' Handbook
ISBN: 978-1-907151-12-5

Girls' Miscellany
ISBN: 978-1-78055-041-1

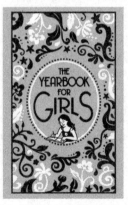

The Yearbook For Girls
ISBN: 978-1-906082-82-6